More Stories of Favorite Operas

More Stories of

BY *Clyde Robert Bulla*

Thomas Y. Crowell Company

Favorite Operas

ILLUSTRATED BY *Joseph Low*

NEW YORK

Books About Opera by the Author

STORIES OF FAVORITE OPERAS

THE RING AND THE FIRE:
Stories from Wagner's Nibelung Operas

MORE STORIES OF FAVORITE OPERAS

1 2 3 4 5 6 7 8 9 10

TO WILLIAM A. PRITCHARD

INTRODUCTORY NOTE

SEVERAL YEARS AGO I retold the stories of twenty-three operas, and the collection was published under the title *Stories of Favorite Operas*. It was hard to limit the number to twenty-three. It was especially hard to omit the four operas in Wagner's "Ring" cycle, and three years later I told the stories of these music dramas in a separate book, *The Ring and the Fire*.

Even before the second book was finished, I was planning a third, which I thought of as *Stories of Favorite Operas Regretfully Omitted from the Two Preceding Books*. Here is the collection, under a more practicable title. The retelling of the stories is meant to help listeners follow the operas with greater understanding and enjoyment.

CONTENTS

More Stories of Favorite Operas

Così fan Tutte

WOLFGANG AMADEUS MOZART *began work on* Così fan Tutte (So Do They All) *in 1789. The story and libretto were by Lorenzo da Ponte, who had also written the librettos of Mozart's earlier operas,* The Marriage of Figaro *and* Don Giovanni.

Così fan Tutte *was first performed in Vienna on January 26, 1790, and before the end of the century it had had performances in many European opera houses, although it did not reach New York until 1922.*

ACT I

IN A CAFE in Naples two young soldiers were having a heated discussion with an elderly bachelor friend. One of the soldiers, Ferrando, loved a lady named Dorabella. The other, Guglielmo, loved her sister, Fiordiligi. Both young men were positive that their sweethearts would always be faithful. The elderly bachelor, Don Alfonso, denied that any woman could be faithful for long, and he offered to convince them that their sweethearts were like all the rest.

"Impossible!" said the young men.

"Shall we bet on it?" asked Don Alfonso. "A hundred sequins?"

Ferrando and Guglielmo agreed.

"You must place yourself in my hands for twenty-four hours," said Don Alfonso. "You must promise to do all I ask and give no sign that will betray our plan."

Again the young men agreed, and they planned how they would spend the hundred sequins.

"I'll hire musicians to serenade my loved one," said Ferrando.

"I'll give a banquet in honor of my beloved," said Guglielmo.

And they decided that Don Alfonso should be invited to witness their triumph.

On that same day Fiordiligi and Dorabella were in the garden of their home by the seashore. Each wore a locket in which was a portrait of her loved one, and as they gazed at the pictures, they talked rapturously of their happiness.

Don Alfonso entered and said in an anguished voice, "Oh, what a terrible day this is, and how I pity you!"

The sisters begged him to tell them what had happened. Were their sweethearts in trouble? Were they dead?

"No, not dead," said Don Alfonso. "They have been ordered to active duty with their regiment."

The sisters were dismayed. "Will they leave without one good-by?" asked Fiordiligi.

"They haven't the courage to face you," said Don Alfonso, "but if you can bear it—" He called to Ferrando and Guglielmo, who were just outside, and the two men came into the garden.

"Heaven help us!" said Guglielmo.

"See how my lips are trembling," said Ferrando.

"You must not leave!" cried Dorabella, and Fiordiligi

declared that she would die at their feet if it would stop their going.

Ferrando whispered triumphantly to Don Alfonso, "What do you say now?" Guglielmo whispered, "Did you hear what they said?"

"The game isn't over," said Don Alfonso.

As if they were summoning all their courage, the soldiers took leave of the ladies. Don Alfonso looked on in secret amusement. "This is an excellent comedy," he said, "and both men are first-rate actors."

A ship had come into the harbor. Soldiers marched to the landing, and townspeople followed to see them sail.

Dorabella clung to Ferrando, telling him he must write to her twice a day. Fiordiligi begged Guglielmo to be true to her. At last the two soldiers tore themselves away and hurried off, pretending they were going to board the ship.

"Poor fellows," said Don Alfonso to himself, "risking a hundred sequins on two women!"

In the house Despina, the maid, had prepared breakfast. The ladies came inside, and she stared at their tragic faces. "What has happened?" she asked.

"A terrible disaster!" said Dorabella.

"Our lovers are gone!" said Fiordiligi.

Despina laughed.

"They are going into battle," said Dorabella.

"They may never come back," said Fiordiligi.

"It would only mean that you had lost two men," said Despina callously. "Consider how many would be left."

"Do you think we could ever love again," said Dorabella, "when we have had two such lovers as these?"

"If you've learned to love one, you can learn to love another," said Despina. "Not that any are worth the trouble." She delivered a lecture on the deceitfulness of men.

The ladies were shocked, and they hurried away. The maid disappeared into her own room.

Don Alfonso entered. He feared Despina might see through his plans and upset them, and he decided to talk with her in secret. He called her and offered her a gold piece. "Take this and listen to me," he said. "You can see your ladies need consolation. Can you find a way to interest them in two suitors who are here from abroad?"

Were they handsome and not too old? asked Despina. Did they have money?

He assured her they were most eligible.

"Bring them in," she said.

He ushered in two gentlemen. They were Ferrando and Guglielmo, disguised in wigs, mustaches, and exotic-look-

ing costumes. "Do your best," Don Alfonso told Despina, and he stepped outside.

Fiordiligi and Dorabella entered and berated the maid for allowing strange men in the house. Despina, Ferrando, and Guglielmo dropped to their knees.

"Please forgive them," said the maid.

"Sweet ladies, we are but two poor creatures who adore you," said the men.

Fiordiligi and Dorabella were outraged.

Don Alfonso came in. "What an uproar! What's the matter?" he asked.

"Look—*men* in our house!" said Dorabella.

"And today of all days!" said Fiordiligi.

Don Alfonso looked at the men. "Good heavens, am I dreaming!" he exclaimed. "My devoted companions!"

"You know these men?" asked Despina.

"They are my two best friends," said Don Alfonso.

"What do they want here?" asked Fiordiligi.

"We come to kneel at your feet and declare our love," said Guglielmo.

"Love has guided us here," said Ferrando.

Fiordiligi ordered them out of the house. In an impassioned speech she declared that she and her sister would be forever faithful to the ones they loved.

"I'd hoped you would show more politeness to my friends," said Don Alfonso.

"Why should we listen to any more?" demanded Fiordiligi.

"Because we suffer so," said Guglielmo. "Your eyes tell us that you suffer, too. If we might comfort one another—" He listed the virtues of his friend and himself. Not only were they loving and tender, but they were strong, healthy, good-humored, and wealthy, and their fine mustaches were symbols of love.

The two ladies swept out of the room, and Despina retired with them.

Guglielmo and Ferrando were triumphant. "We've won the bet!" they said.

"Not so fast," said Don Alfonso. "Remember your bargain. You must obey me until tomorrow morning." He sent them outside to await his next order, then he called Despina and asked what word she had of the ladies.

"They are despairing and complaining now," she said, "but I'll change their way of thinking."

"How can you manage it?" he asked.

"Bring the two fellows to me," said Despina. "I have a plan."

Dorabella and Fiordiligi were in the garden, lamenting their fate. Life had been so beautiful. Now it was a sea of torment. Voices came from behind the shrubbery.

"There may be hope," Don Alfonso was saying. "Oh, please don't do it!"

"Don't try to stop us!" said Ferrando and Guglielmo. They came into the open. As Don Alfonso came running after them, they drank from the small flasks they carried.

"Heavens!" cried the ladies. "Have they taken poison?"

"Yes," said Don Alfonso, "and in a short time they will be dead."

The ladies called for help. Despina came out of the house and looked at the two men, who were lying on the grass. She said to Don Alfonso, "Come with me. We'll try

to find a doctor." They rushed off together. Fiordiligi and Dorabella stood helplessly by. The men had begun to groan.

"We can't leave them in such a state," said Fiordiligi.

"They have quite interesting faces," said her sister.

They felt the men's foreheads and pulsebeats and told each other that if help did not come soon, the poor young men would be gone.

Don Alfonso returned with a strange-looking figure— Despina in disguise—whom he introduced as a doctor. The pretended doctor produced a huge magnet and applied it to the young men's foreheads. The men began to stir, as if waking from a dream. Ferrando gazed into Fiordiligi's face. Guglielmo gazed up at Dorabella.

"Have pity, my darling!" sighed the men.

"Don't be alarmed at what they say," said Despina. "These are just the after-effects of the poison."

The men begged for kisses from the ladies.

"They need confidence," said Despina and Don Alfonso. "It will help them."

But both ladies firmly refused to go to the gentlemen's aid.

ACT II

Despina, Fiordiligi, and Dorabella were talking in a room of the sisters' home. Despina was pleading the cause of the two young men.

"What you took for audacity was the effect of the poison," she explained. "I'm sure they have recovered by now."

"What do you think we should do?" asked Fiordiligi.

"Do as your heart tells you," said Despina, and she left the ladies to make their decision.

"She seems a little crazy," said Fiordiligi, "but—have you thought of taking her advice?"

"She told us we'd be doing no harm," said Dorabella.

"What if our lovers found out?" asked Fiordiligi.

"They needn't find out," said Dorabella, "and we'll still be faithful to them. This will be only an amusement to make us forget our grief."

Fiordiligi agreed.

"Well, then—" said Dorabella. For herself she chose the dark-haired man. Fiordiligi preferred the blond one. Now that their minds were made up, they looked forward to a daring yet harmless diversion.

Don Alfonso called to invite them to a garden party. "It's quite a brilliant spectacle," he said. "Come and join us."

At the party servants were hurrying about and musicians were playing. Despina was there. Ferrando and Guglielmo, in their disguises, were singing a love song. Don Alfonso and Despina led them forward to greet Dorabella and Fiordiligi.

Don Alfonso felt that the ladies and gentlemen were much too shy, and he and Despina undertook to give them a lesson in proper behavior, then they left the two couples alone.

Fiordiligi and Ferrando strolled off to another part of the garden.

Guglielmo offered Dorabella a gift—a heart-shaped locket —in token of his affection. She was not free to accept it, she told him.

"I adore you," he said. "If you reject me, I shall perish!" Again he offered his gift. This time she accepted it, and he hung the heart-shaped locket about her neck, taking in return her locket in which she carried Ferrando's picture. They left, arm in arm.

Fiordiligi entered, with Ferrando pursuing her.

"Why do you run away?" he asked.

She answered that she had seen evil in him. She commanded him to leave her.

"Ah, you are smiling and sighing!" he said, and he warned her dramatically that if they were ever parted he would die.

After he had gone Fiordiligi reproached herself for having listened to anything the stranger had to say. As she went away, Ferrando and Guglielmo came out into the garden.

"We've won our bet," said Ferrando. "Fiordiligi is completely true to you."

"You are a faithful friend to bring me the news," said Guglielmo.

"What of Dorabella?" asked Ferrando. "Not that I have any doubts about her."

"A few doubts may be in order," said Guglielmo.

"What do you mean?" asked Ferrando. "She loves no one but me."

"Of course," said Guglielmo ironically, "and to prove it, she gave me this." He displayed Dorabella's locket.

Ferrando was stricken.

"Why upset yourself over someone who isn't worth it?" said Guglielmo, and he left his friend alone in the garden.

For a time Ferrando was shaken by anger and thoughts of revenge. Then he admitted to himself that he still loved Dorabella as much as before.

Guglielmo and Don Alfonso returned.

"As I understand it," said Don Alfonso, "Fiordiligi has been true to Guglielmo and Dorabella has not been true to Ferrando."

"Yes, to my shame," said Ferrando.

"The two cases are quite different," said Guglielmo complacently. "I'm not conceited, but you must admit that I have a certain advantage. So now that I have won half the bet, will you please pay me?"

"Before I do, I'll ask for one more test," said Don Alfonso. "Don't forget that our bet lasts until tomorrow, and you've promised on your honor to obey me until then."

Back in the house Dorabella and Despina were comparing notes on the exciting events of the day.

"I couldn't resist the charming fellow," Dorabella confessed.

"Now you're behaving sensibly," said Despina. "It isn't

often we poor women meet a man who's worth while, so when one does happen along, we ought to make the most of it."

Fiordiligi entered. All the world seemed to have gone mad, she said. Now she was in love, not with Guglielmo, but with the handsome blond foreigner.

Dorabella was delighted. "Then we can both be married," she said, "you to the blond-haired man, I to the black-haired one!"

"How could we change our minds in just one day?" said Fiordiligi.

"A ridiculous question. We're women, aren't we?" said Dorabella. She added that it was futile to try to resist love.

She and Despina went away together. Fiordiligi did not follow them. "I'll die before I give in!" she vowed. An idea came to her. She and her sister would dress in soldiers' uniforms and go to the battle front in search of their sweethearts.

She called the maid and sent her for the uniforms Guglielmo and Ferrando had stored in the house. Despina brought the uniforms, muttering that her lady had surely lost her senses.

Fiordiligi threw aside her headdress and put on a soldier's helmet. "Ah, how this transforms me! Now I go to my beloved!" she said.

Ferrando was listening in the doorway. He came forward. "If you leave, it will kill me," he said.

She ordered him to go.

He pleaded with her. Little by little he overcame her resistance, until she was in his arms. He led her away.

Guglielmo and Don Alfonso had been spying from the doorway. Guglielmo was incredulous. "Poor creature that I am, that this should happen to me!" he said.

Ferrando entered.

"Where is she?" shouted Guglielmo.

"Do you mean Fiordiligi? You have nothing to fear," said Ferrando with heavy irony. "Remember, you have a certain advantage."

"Oh, stop tormenting me," groaned Guglielmo. "The important thing now is to take revenge on these two creatures."

"I know a way," said Don Alfonso. "Marry them."

"I'd rather marry the devil's grandmother," said Guglielmo.

"Or a female dragon," said Ferrando.

Don Alfonso asked them, "Would you rather be lonely bachelors?"

"There are plenty of women," said Ferrando.

"But do you think they would be any different?" asked

Don Alfonso. "Why not admit it? You still love your unfaithful sweethearts."

"Yes, we love them, we love them," said Guglielmo and
Ferrando miserably.

"Then," said Don Alfonso, "you must take them as they

are. Why should you expect nature to create two special exceptions just for you? The best way to assure your happiness is to see that you are married as soon as possible."

Despina came to tell them that the two ladies had agreed to a wedding. She was arranging the details, and a notary would be there to draw up the contract. "Does this make you happy?" she asked.

"Ecstatically!" answered the three men.

In a richly decorated hall preparations for the wedding were being made. An orchestra had assembled. A table was set. Despina was ordering the servants about. Don Alfonso entered and approved of all that had been done. Then, hinting at some mysterious mission, he led Despina away.

The bridal party was ushered into the hall. The two bridegrooms with their ladies sat down to the wedding supper.

Don Alfonso returned and announced that it was time for the signing of the marriage contract. He called the notary, and Despina appeared, disguised in a white wig and a dark cloak. In a nasal voice she began to read the contract. The two couples stopped her, saying they preferred to sign it now and read it later.

The two ladies signed the paper. The two men avoided putting their names to it.

As Don Alfonso took charge of the document, there was a commotion outside. Villagers were singing a song of welcome to the regiment. Don Alfonso looked out the window. "What a catastrophe!" he said. "Here are your former lovers!"

The musicians fled. Servants rushed back and forth, removing the wedding decorations.

The brides pushed Ferrando and Guglielmo out of sight through a doorway. Don Alfonso thrust the disguised Despina into another room. He tried to soothe the terrified ladies, but they would not be calmed. Over and over they asked themselves what would happen if their lovers learned the truth.

Ferrando and Guglielmo came striding in, dressed in their army uniforms.

"My friends, back so quickly!" Don Alfonso greeted them.

The two soldiers explained that their plans had been changed. They had been ordered back to Naples.

"We are overjoyed to be with our dear ones again," said Ferrando.

Guglielmo asked Fiordiligi, "Why so pale and silent?"

Ferrando asked Dorabella, "Why do you look so sad?"

Don Alfonso spoke for the ladies. "They are speechless with astonishment," he said.

"Excuse me while I put away my knapsack," said Guglielmo, opening a door. "Who's this? A notary?"

The maid came out. "I am not a notary, only Despina," she said. "I've just come from a masquerade."

Fiordiligi and Dorabella were bewildered. "Despina?" they said. "How could it be Despina?"

Don Alfonso let the marriage contract fall from his hand.

"What's this?" asked Ferrando, picking up the paper.

"A marriage contract!" said Guglielmo.

He and Ferrando turned on the ladies. "You've signed the paper," they said. "You can't deny it."

Weeping, the ladies admitted their guilt. "They are the traitors," they said, pointing to Despina and Don Alfonso. "They led us into this."

"That is true," said Don Alfonso. "You'll find the proof in there."

The two soldiers went into the next room. In a few moments they were back, wearing parts of their former disguises. Ferrando bowed to Fiordiligi and said in an exaggerated imitation of a foreign nobleman, "Lovely lady, I kneel before you. I am a knight arrived from Albania."

Guglielmo said to Dorabella, "Here is a locket that came from you."

The two soldiers congratulated Despina on her performance as the magnetic physician.

Now the deception was clear to the ladies. When they found their voices, they tried to place the blame on Don Alfonso.

"I admit my guilt," he said, "but it was only to teach you lovers a lesson in the ways of women."

The two ladies asked the men's forgiveness. Ferrando and Guglielmo gladly forgave them, and the two couples, Don Alfonso, and Despina agreed that he is happy who can be cheerful in the face of things that bring unhappiness to others—when he has learned that sorrow will turn to joy another day.

Fidelio

FIDELIO, *Ludwig van Beethoven's only opera, was composed to a libretto by Josef Sonnleithner. The story was based on the text of a French opera, Léonore, which had been produced in Paris a few years earlier.*

Fidelio was first given in Vienna on November 20, 1805, when the city was occupied by Napoleon's army and the whole country was suffering from an economic depression. The performance was a failure.

Shortened and remodeled, the work was again produced in Vienna a few months later. The new version met with some success, but Beethoven and the theater manager quarreled, and the composer withdrew his opera after five performances. Fidelio was successfully revived in Vienna in the spring of 1814.

ACT I

IN EIGHTEENTH-CENTURY Spain the State Prison was a grim and forbidding fortress near Seville. Within the prison walls lived Rocco, the jailer, and his daughter, Marzelline. Young Jaquino, the turnkey and porter, also lived within the walls.

One spring day Marzelline was ironing linen in the courtyard just outside her door. Jaquino came by. Happy

to find her alone, he began making love to her and asking when they might be married.

The girl was relieved when her father called Jaquino away. Once she might have encouraged the young man. Now someone else had come into her life—Fidelio, her father's new assistant.

Jaquino returned, carrying a load of garden tools. Rocco was with him. The jailer looked about for Fidelio, who had been sent out on several errands.

There was a knocking, and Jaquino unlocked the door. The assistant entered, heavily burdened with a basket of provisions, an armload of chains, and a tin box containing letters.

Rocco looked over the bill his assistant had brought back. "Well done," he said. "In six months you have saved more than I could save in a year. You are a worthy lad, and you shall be rewarded." He glanced significantly toward his daughter.

The assistant looked away in confusion. What Rocco did not know—what no one else in the prison knew or suspected—was that the name, Fidelio, was part of a disguise. The assistant was actually a woman, Lady Leonore.

Her husband, Florestan, had disappeared two years before. One of his most dangerous political enemies was Pizarro, overseer of the State Prison, and Leonore believed it was he who had caused her husband's disappearance. Disguised as a man, she had come to the prison, hoping to find some trace of Florestan.

Rocco's daughter had fallen in love with the gentle, well-bred Fidelio. Rocco had further complicated matters by approving the match.

Now, looking benevolently on the two young people, the jailer told them, "You know that our overseer goes every month to Seville to give a report on the prison. Soon he will be off again, and the day after he leaves will be a good time to have you married."

Marzelline was ecstatic. Leonore tried to hide her dismay.

Rocco offered a word of fatherly advice. Love was all very well, but a happy family also needed money.

"There is something else I should prize just as much," said Leonore. "Something I have not yet been able to gain."

"What is that?" asked Rocco.

"Your confidence," said Leonore. "Sometimes when you come up from the dungeons, you are almost exhausted. Why won't you let me go with you? I should be so glad if I could help you there."

"You know my orders," he said. "I can let no one go near the state prisoners."

"But there are too many prisoners," said Marzelline. "You work yourself to death."

"We should spare ourselves a little for those who love us," said Leonore.

Rocco agreed that they were right. "The overseer is a severe man," he said, "but he will surely allow me to take you into the secret dungeons."

Leonore could not hold back a gesture of elation.

"But," said Rocco, "there is one cell into which you may not go."

"Is this the cell of the prisoner I sometimes hear you mention?" asked Marzelline.

"You have guessed it," answered her father.

"I believe he has been here a long time," said Leonore.
"More than two years," said Rocco.

"Two years!" exclaimed Leonore. Then she forced herself to speak calmly, "He must be a great criminal."

"Or have great enemies," said Rocco. "It amounts to the same thing."

"No one knows his name or where he comes from?" asked Marzelline.

"He has tried often enough to tell me, but I've never listened. In my position it's better to know as few secrets as possible," said Rocco. "Well, he won't trouble me much longer, poor fellow." By Pizarro's order the prisoner's rations were being steadily decreased. For the past twenty-four hours he had been given only two ounces of black bread and a half-measure of water.

Martial music sounded, heralding Pizarro's arrival. Leonore quickly handed Rocco the tin box of letters, and she and Marzelline went into the jailer's house.

Pizarro came into the courtyard, leading a detachment of soldiers. Rocco delivered the letters to him, and the overseer looked through them. One was an unsigned warning: "I inform you what the Minister has learned—that several of your prisoners are the victims of arbitrary power. He leaves tomorrow to surprise you with an investigation. Be on your guard."

Pizarro read the message in consternation. According to the date of the letter, "tomorrow" meant that the investigation would be today. The Minister believed his friend, Florestan, to be long dead. What if Florestan were found here, alive and able to speak out against his enemies?

Pizarro swiftly decided what must be done. He called

the captain of the guards and ordered him to take one of the trumpeters into the tower. "Watch the road to Seville," he said. "If you see the Minister's carriage, let me hear a signal instantly."

The captain went away, and Pizarro summoned Rocco. From the doorway of the jailer's house Leonore looked on her husband's enemy with dread and loathing.

Pizarro spoke to the jailer with false geniality, "Now, my friend, good luck has come to you. Here—this is only the start." He gave Rocco a purse.

"Let me know how I can serve you," said the jailer.

"Your long service has made you a man of courage," said Pizarro.

"What must I do?" asked Rocco.

"Murder," said Pizarro.

Rocco drew back, and Pizzaro said furiously, "Are you a man? There is no time to hesitate. A prisoner of state must die."

Rocco protested that he had not been hired to kill.

"I'll do it if your courage fails," said Pizarro. "Go quickly to the certain prisoner. You know the one. Dig a grave in his cell."

"And then?" asked Rocco.

"Give a signal, and I'll be there," said Pizarro, showing Rocco a dagger. "One blow, and all will be finished."

Rocco was horrified, yet he agreed to the plan, thinking that death might be a merciful release to the poor prisoner.

Pizarro went out into the prison garden, and Rocco followed. Leonore stepped from the doorway where she had been watching the overseer. "Monstrous fiend!" she cried. "Neither pity nor the voice of humanity can move your heart!" Yet she clung to her hope, and she resolved to be strong for whatever ordeal might come.

She left in search of Rocco.

Marzelline and Jaquino came out of the jailer's house. She would listen no more to his talk of love, she was saying, while he reminded her bitterly, "Once I was your dear Jaquino, but now that Fidelio is here—"

"I won't deny that I liked you," she said, "but my feelings for Fidelio are different."

Fidelio was a vagabond, said Jaquino. Her father had taken him in only out of pity.

"And I shall marry him for all that!" said Marzelline.

Leonore and Rocco entered, and the jailer put an end to the quarrel. "Think no more of my daughter," he told Jaquino. "I have a more sensible plan."

"I understand, father," said Marzelline fondly.

Leonore quickly changed the subject. She asked if some of the prisoners might be allowed to walk in the garden.

"Not without the overseer's permission," said Rocco.

"Perhaps you can do him some favor," suggested Marzelline. "Then he will not mind."

"A favor? You are right," said Rocco. "I'll risk it."

He went to find Pizarro. Leonore and Jaquino opened the prison gates. Slowly, a few at a time, the ragged, unkempt figures emerged from their cells. Accustomed to darkness, they shielded their eyes from the light, and in hushed voices they spoke to one another of their joy at breathing the pure air again. They moved on into the garden, and Marzelline and Jaquino followed them.

Rocco returned and told Leonore that he had talked with Pizarro. Not only had the overseer consented to the

marriage of Marzelline and Fidelio, but he had agreed that
Fidelio might help the jailer in the dungeons. "This very
day you shall go with me to the prisoner of whom we
have spoken," he said.

Leonore asked, "Is he to be set free?"

"He will have his freedom," answered Rocco, "but in
the grave."

"Then he is dead?" she asked.

"Not yet," said the jailer.

She asked in horror, "Are you bound to kill this man?"

"No," said Rocco. "I am no murderer. The overseer himself will go down there. You and I have only to dig the
grave."

"Perhaps the grave of my husband," thought Leonore,
and Rocco, glancing anxiously at his young assistant, said
to himself, "I think he weeps."

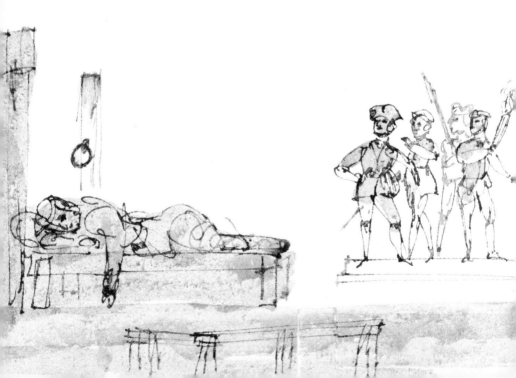

Marzelline and Jaquino appeared. They had seen Pizarro. He was furious, they said, because the prisoners had been allowed in the garden without his permission.

Pizarro stormed into the courtyard. "What rights are you taking on yourself?" he shouted.

Rocco humbly offered his excuses. The weather was fine. It was the king's birthday. He added in a low voice that since one prisoner was to die, it could surely do no harm to show a small mercy to the others.

"Then go dig the grave," said Pizarro.

The prisoners came from the garden, bidding farewell to the sunlight. They returned to their cells. Leonore and Jaquino locked the gate behind them.

ACT II

A lamp burned dimly in the dungeon, where a man sat chained to the wall. He was the mysterious prisoner of state, Florestan.

He cried out against the gloom and silence. He recalled a time when his life had been joyful and free and he had dared to speak boldly against wrong. In a kind of exaltation he called up an image of an angel on earth. He spoke her name, "Leonore, Leonore, my beloved wife!"

For a little while it seemed to him that she was really there, leading him to freedom and happiness. Then, exhausted, he sank back on the stones.

Rocco and Leonore came down the stairway, carrying a lantern, a pitcher of wine, and tools for digging. Leonore tried to see the prisoner's face.

"He may be dead," said Rocco.

"Do you think so?" she asked, shuddering.

The prisoner moved slightly. Rocco said, "No, he is sleeping." He pointed out an old cistern, no longer used, that was to be the prisoner's grave. The opening was covered with earth and stones. "We need not dig far," he said. "Give me a pickaxe."

Leonore was trembling.

"Are you afraid?" he asked.

"No," said Leonore, "only—it is so cold."

While they dug out earth and lifted the stones, she kept turning to look at the motionless prisoner.

Rocco paused to rest and drank from the pitcher. The prisoner awakened and lifted his head. Rocco asked him, "Have you rested?"

"How could I rest?" said the prisoner.

"That voice!" said Leonore to herself.

"Man of stone, will you always be deaf to me?" said the prisoner, turning a little. Leonore saw his face. "God in heaven, it is he!" she cried, and fell fainting beside the grave.

Rocco asked the prisoner, "What do you want of me? I only carry out my orders."

"Can you tell me who is overseer of this prison?" asked Florestan.

The name could be revealed now without risk, thought Rocco, and he answered that the overseer was Pizarro.

Leonore had regained consciousness. She heard the prisoner say, "Send quickly to Seville. Ask there for Leonore Florestan."

"Impossible," said Rocco. "It would only ruin me, without helping you." But his heart was touched. He offered to give the prisoner what was left of the wine.

Leonore brought the pitcher. "Who is that?" asked Florestan.

"My assistant, and soon to be my son-in-law," answered Rocco.

Florestan drank the wine. Leonore took a crust of bread from her pocket and gave it to him. He blessed her for her goodness.

The cistern was open. Rocco went to the back of the cell and whistled—the signal that was to bring Pizarro.

Florestan asked, "Is that the signal for my death?"

"No, no! Try to calm yourself," said Leonore, "and whatever happens, never forget that there is a God in heaven."

Pizarro entered, enveloped in a long, dark cloak. His face was half-hidden, and he spoke in a disguised voice, "Is everything ready?"

"Yes," said Rocco.

"Good," said Pizarro. "The boy must go."

Rocco ordered Leonore to leave. She withdrew into the shadows, but gradually she crept forward again.

Pizarro told himself that he must next be rid of the jailer and the boy, so that Florestan's murder could never come to light.

"Shall I take off the prisoner's chains?" asked Rocco.

"No, but unfasten them from the stone," said Pizarro. Gloating in his hatred, he drew his dagger and looked down on the prisoner. He threw off his cloak and revealed himself. "Pizarro, the avenger, stands before you."

Florestan answered steadily, "A murderer stands before me."

Pizarro raised the dagger. Before he could strike, Leonore sprang forward and placed herself between him and Florestan.

Pizarro threw her aside. Again he lifted the dagger, and again Leonore shielded Florestan.

"First kill his wife!" she said.

"His wife!" exclaimed Pizarro and Rocco.

She said to Florestan, "I am Leonore."

"Leonore!" he cried.

"You have shared his life," said Pizarro, "now share his doom!"

Leonore drew a pistol from her doublet. "Another word and you are dead!" she said.

At that moment a trumpet call sounded from high in the tower—the signal Pizarro had ordered, to warn him that the Minister was approaching the prison.

The trumpet sounded again. Jaquino, followed by soldiers bearing torches, appeared on the stairs. He called down that the Minister and his guards were at the gate.

"We are coming!" answered Rocco.

Pizarro, cursing his ill-fortune, rushed off. Rocco followed him. Leonore and Florestan were left alone together, joyously reunited.

In the courtyard a welcome ceremony had been prepared for the Minister, Don Fernando. The prison guards marched in and formed an open square. From one side came the Minister and Pizarro. From the other side came Jaquino, Marzelline, and the prisoners.

Rocco, Leonore, and Florestan made their way through the crowd. The jailer appealed to Don Fernando, "Have pity on this hapless pair."

The Minister was astonished to recognize his friend Florestan, whom he had thought dead.

"And Leonore," said Rocco. "She came here—"

Pizarro tried to interrupt. The Minister ordered him to be silent.

Rocco continued, telling how Leonore had entered his service as a hireling boy.

Jaquino listened with elation, but Marzelline was in tears.

Rocco indicated Pizarro. "Within the hour," he said, "this man sought to murder Florestan."

The Minister called for Florestan's release and Pizarro's arrest. Guards seized Pizarro and led him away.

Florestan was still in chains. Don Fernando told Rocco, "Take off his chains. But wait." He said to Leonore, "It is more fitting that you should set him completely free."

He gave her the keys. In the midst of great rejoicing, she unlocked her husband's chains and took him in her arms.

Der Freischütz

CARL MARIA VON WEBER, *in 1810, found the story of* Der Freischütz (The Freeshooter) *in a collection of supernatural tales. At once he saw it as the subject for an opera, and seven years later his friend Friedrich Kind supplied the libretto.*

Weber finished the score in 1820. Der Freischütz *had its first performance in Berlin on June 18, 1821, and was a spectacular success. Up until then, Italian influence had dominated the operatic scene in Germany.* Der Freischütz *opened the way to a new and typically German school of opera.*

ACT I

IN THE MIDDLE of the seventeenth century Bohemia was a nation of hunters. Huntsmen stalked game in every forest. Wherever people gathered, they talked of weapons and the hunt. Expert marksmanship was honored and highly prized.

During Prince Ottokar's reign a worthy man named Cuno was Chief Huntsman of Bohemia. By tradition the title passed from father to son, but Cuno had no son. His daughter, Agathe, was betrothed to Max, a promising young hunter and marksman. Since Cuno was preparing to step aside for someone younger, he had asked that his son-in-law succeed him. Prince Ottokar had agreed, provided Max could pass the required test.

A preliminary match was held. All Max's skill seemed to have deserted him. Outside a tavern in the woods he sat at a table and watched while Kilian, a common peasant, fired at the target and outshot him.

After his victory Kilian and his friends paraded past

Max, jeering and bowing mockingly. Max was aroused at last. He leaped up and attacked the boastful peasant.

Cuno appeared with a group of his huntsmen. Among them was Caspar, who was generally known as an idler and a ne'er-do-well.

"What's the matter here?" asked Cuno.

Kilian answered that no harm had been intended. "With us," he said, "it's the custom to have a little fun with the fellow who misses every shot."

"Who missed every shot?" asked Cuno.

Max admitted that he had not been able to hit the target even once.

Caspar said under his breath, "Thanks, Samiel!" It was he who had spoiled Max's aim by casting a spell on him. This he had done with the aid of Samiel, the evil and supernatural Black Huntsman, who inhabited the forest.

Caspar said to Max with pretended concern, "Somebody must have bewitched you. If you will call on the Black Huntsman to break the spell—"

"Silence!" interrupted Cuno. "I know you for a cheat and a drunkard. Take care, lest I think even worse of you." For Max, too, he had a warning, but a kindlier one. "You must be careful. If you fail in the trial shot tomorrow, my daughter's hand cannot be yours."

Some of the men asked him to tell them about the trial shot.

He told the story. Long ago his great-great-grandfather, the first Cuno, was hunting with the prince. The dogs started a stag on whose back a man had been bound—a common punishment for poachers in those days. The sight distressed the prince. He promised to reward anyone who could bring down the stag without wounding the man. The first Cuno tried. It was a difficult shot, but he succeeded. In return the prince gave him the title of Chief Huntsman and a hunting lodge of his own. But jealous tongues spread the rumor that the first Cuno had made the shot unfairly, that the bullet had been guided by black magic.

Kilian told his friends that he had heard of these magic bullets. They were molded seven at a time with the help of Samiel, the Evil One. Six would hit any mark. The seventh belonged to Samiel, who could guide it wherever he wished. "Free" bullets, they were called, and the hunter who used them was a "freeshooter."

Cuno finished his story. The first Cuno had won his position with expert marksmanship. Since then each man to inherit the title had passed the test of the trial shot.

Max's test was set for the next day. Cuno and the other huntsmen offered him encouragement before they went on their way. Kilian, too, wished him good luck and invited him into the tavern.

But Max was in no mood for dancing or gaiety, and Kilian and the other peasants went into the tavern without him.

Left alone, Max reflected on his doubts and fears. Out of the shadows behind him rose a hulking figure with a sinister, yellow face. It was Samiel, the Black Huntsman. Unseen, he moved forward in great, slow strides.

Max seemed to feel the breath of evil, and he prayed for help. Hearing the word "God," Samiel shuddered violently and disappeared.

Caspar returned—to console his comrade, he said. He

ordered wine, poured some for Max, and secretly added something from a phial.

"Help, Samiel!" he muttered, and the Black Huntsman peered out from among the bushes.

Max insisted he wanted no wine, but he could not graciously refuse to drink when Caspar proposed a toast to Cuno. Neither could he refuse when Caspar proposed a toast to Agathe, then to Prince Ottokar.

Dusk had come. A clock struck seven. It was time for Max to go, but Caspar kept him there with mysterious half-promises: "There are certain tricks I might tell you, and on this night, when the moon is in eclipse, great things may be accomplished."

Samiel appeared, listening. He faded from sight, and appeared again.

"What if I should help you make the most fortunate kind of shot?" asked Caspar. "A shot that would quiet Agathe's fears and assure your success tomorrow?"

"How could that be?" asked Max.

Caspar thrust his rifle into Max's hands. "There! See that eagle yonder? Fire!"

Max was annoyed. "Do you take me for a fool? The bird is only a tiny spot, far out of range."

"Fire, in the devil's name!" Caspar commanded him.

Max touched the trigger. The eagle fell dead at his feet.

"Victory!" said Caspar. He plucked out some of the eagle's feathers and stuck them in Max's hatband.

Max was staring at the bird in bewilderment. He asked, "What kind of bullet was that?"

"Are you so ignorant?" said Caspar. "Don't you really know?"

"The shot was incredible," said Max. "Have you any more of those bullets?"

It was the only one left, Caspar told him. However, there were more to be had.

"How can I get one?" asked Max.

"Be in Wolf's Glen at midnight," said Caspar.

Wolf's Glen was well known as a place of evil enchantment. "No," said Max. "I shall not come."

"Coward!" said Caspar. "Only through danger can you win your reward." He went on, with terrible earnestness. What if Max failed to win Agathe's hand? What if Agathe died of loneliness and Max died of grief and shame? He pretended to weep, while muttering behind his hand, "Help, Samiel!"

Max decided suddenly. "By Agathe's life, I'll come!" he said.

ACT II

Agathe and her cousin Aennchen were together in Cuno's hunting lodge. Aennchen was hanging a picture that had fallen from the wall—a portrait of the first Cuno. The falling picture had struck Agathe and injured her, although not seriously.

Aennchen complained humorously of the loneliness of the old house. It was certainly disagreeable, she said, to be in such a place at night, especially when departed ancestors took it into their heads to come down off the wall. "For my part," she said, "I prefer live men and younger ones."

She talked of the wedding she would have some day and how happy she would be to wear the bridal wreath.

"Who knows?" said Agathe. "A bridal wreath may have its thorns." But she had felt less melancholy since visiting the Hermit that morning, she told her cousin. The holy man had given her some consecrated roses. At the same time he had warned her of danger. "You can see how his words have been fulfilled," she said. "That falling picture might have killed me."

Aennchen offered to put the roses out in the cool night air so that they would last longer. "Then let us go to bed," she said.

"Not until I have seen Max," said Agathe, and Aennchen went out, carrying the flowers.

Agathe mused on love and sorrow, wondering why the two so often went hand in hand. As she gazed out at the stars, she prayed that heaven would protect her.

Max came in sight. She looked for a nosegay on his hat— the sign that he had won the shooting contest. He greeted her, and she drew back in disappointment. Instead of flowers on his hat, there were eagle feathers.

He began to talk feverishly of his luck in bringing down a great eagle. Then he noticed the wound on her forehead, and he asked what had happened.

Aennchen had come back, and she explained. At seven o'clock Agathe had gone to the window to look for him. The picture had fallen and struck her head.

"Strange," said Max. "Just at that time I shot the eagle."

"You are talking to yourself. What is wrong?" asked Agathe.

Max denied that anything was wrong. In fact, he said, he had had even more good luck. "At dusk I shot a large stag," he said, unable to meet her eyes as he spoke. "I must bring him in now before he is stolen."

"Where did the stag fall?"asked Agathe.

"In Wolf's Glen," said Max.

Agathe and Aennchen were horrified at the idea of his going there—especially at night, with a storm coming on.

"I must go," he said. "A huntsman must have courage." He took up his hat and rifle, but before he left, he asked Agathe if she forgave him for his strangeness tonight.

"Yes," she answered. "My heart forgives you."

Wolf's Glen was a weird, craggy hollow surrounded by mountains. A cascade plunged over the rocks. Thunder sounded a long way off, and invisible spirits chanted and cried.

While Caspar waited in the glen, he had been placing black stones in a circle. In the middle of the circle was a skull. Nearby were a ladle, a bullet mold, and an eagle's wing.

Far in the distance a clock struck twelve. Caspar thrust his broadsword into the skull.

"Samiel, Samiel, appear!" he called.

The Black Huntsman rose from among the rocks and asked, "Why do you call me?"

"You know why," said Caspar. He had sold himself to the Evil One. Tomorrow his time on earth would end, unless he could bring Samiel another victim. He had plotted to deliver Max to Samiel—not only to save himself, but because he hated Max. Once Caspar had loved Agathe, and she had rejected him.

A brave and gallant youth was on the way, he told Samiel.

"What does he seek?" asked the Black Huntsman.

"Only bullets that you shall guide," said Caspar.

"Six bullets will be for him," said Samiel.

"The seventh will be for you, to slay his bride," said Caspar eagerly. "Her death will drive him mad."

Samiel answered that as yet he had no power over the girl, but he agreed that, in exchange for the young man, he would grant Caspar three more years on earth.

Thunder crashed, and the Black Huntsman disappeared.

Caspar saw that the sword and skull had vanished. In their place was a glowing hearth. He fanned the coals with the eagle's wing until the fire blazed up.

Max appeared on a rocky point opposite the cascade. A ghostly apparition floated before him—the figure of his mother clothed in white.

"She warns me to go back!" said Max.

"Help, Samiel!" said Caspar, and he called up to Max, laughing at him for being afraid.

The white-clad figure faded, and a vision of Agathe took its place. With gestures of madness, she seemed about to throw herself into the cascade.

"I must follow her!" cried Max, but as he leaped down over the rocks, the image vanished. He stopped near the circle of stones. "Here I am," he said. "What would you have me do?"

"First drink," said Caspar. "Then you will cast the bullets."

Max drank from the flask Caspar offered, but he refused to cast the bullets. "That was not in the agreement," he said.

"Stand firm, then. Do not shrink at whatever you see or hear," said Caspar, "but if I tremble, come close to me and repeat whatever I call."

He set quickly to work. He took up the ladle and threw into it some lead and evil charms. The mixture began to boil. A shadow darkened the moon.

Caspar tipped the ladle and poured the first bullet into the mold.

"One!" he said, and an echo repeated the word. Wild birds swooped down over the fire.

He cast the next bullet. "Two!" he said, and the word echoed. A wild boar rushed out of the wood and went crashing away through the bushes.

Caspar hesitated, then cast the third bullet. "Three!" he said. "Three! Three!" came the echo. A storm broke, whipping the treetops and scattering sparks from the fire.

"Four!" said Caspar, and he cast another bullet. The echo sounded, along with the beat of horses' hoofs. Fiery wheels came rattling over the rocks.

He cast the fifth bullet and shouted, "Five!" The echoed word came back, "Five! Five!" There was a burst of wild music, during which skeleton dogs and hunters were seen pursuing a stag through the air.

"Six! Oh, horror!" cried Caspar. "Six! Oh, horror!" repeated the echo. Meteors streamed across the sky. Flames rose from the earth. Rain fell in torrents, and a tempest lashed the earth.

Caspar lifted his voice. "Samiel, hear me! Seven, Samiel!" The storm threw him to the ground.

"Samiel!" shouted Max.

A terrible voice spoke, "I am here," and the Black Huntsman was there, grasping Max's hand. Convulsively Max made the sign of the cross. In an instant Samiel was gone and silence had fallen.

ACT III

Agathe, wearing her wedding gown, knelt at the altar in her room. On the altar were the white roses given to her by the Hermit. Aennchen entered. She, too, was dressed for the wedding. "How sad you seem," she said. "You have been weeping."

"Max must have been out in the storm last night," said Agathe, "and I have had fearful dreams." She had dreamed she was changed to a white dove. Max fired at her and she fell. Then she was herself again, and a great bird of prey lay dead beside her.

Aennchen undertook to interpret the dream. The white dove was the wedding gown. The black feathers in Max's hat had suggested the bird of prey.

To put Agathe in a more cheerful frame of mind, Aennchen told her a ridiculous tale of an old aunt who had been startled out of a half-dream by the sight of a monster with rattling chains and burning eyes. When servants came to rescue her, the monster turned out to be the family watchdog!

She went away to bring the bridal wreath that had been sent out from the village. The bridesmaids came to wish Agathe happiness.

Aennchen returned with word that the portrait of the first Cuno had fallen again. To Agathe this was another bad omen. Aennchen laughed at her fears. In a playful little ceremony, she knelt and presented the box that had come from the village.

Agathe opened it and gave a cry. Inside the box was a funeral wreath.

In spite of herself Aennchen was frightened, although she tried to hide her alarm. "The old lady put in the wrong wreath," she said. "Whatever shall we do?"

Agathe decided to wear the flowers from the altar. Aennchen wove them into a wreath, which she set on Agathe's hair. Then she and the bridesmaids led the bride away.

The tents of Prince Ottokar and his party had been pitched in a wooded spot. On one side the prince was feasting. Cuno was at the table, and Max stood near him. On the other side, lurking behind a tree, was Caspar.

Prince Ottokar announced that serious business was at hand. Cuno signaled Max to be ready for the trial shot.

Caspar muttered, "Help, Samiel!" and climbed into the tree for a better view of the proceedings.

Prince Ottokar asked why Agathe was not there. Cuno answered that she was on her way, but he suggested that Max make the trial shot before she came. With the bride present, the young man might not shoot so well.

The prince agreed that this might be true. In a preliminary test that morning Max had fired three master shots, but since then he had seemed strangely nervous.

Max came forward. The "free" bullets had been divided— four to him, three to Caspar. In the earlier test Max had used three of his bullets. Now he was prepared to fire the one that was left.

"Shoot as you did this morning, and you have nothing to fear," Prince Ottokar told him. "See the white dove yonder? That should be an easy shot. Fire!"

As Max raised his rifle, Agathe, Aennchen, and the bridesmaids came in sight. "Do not fire!" cried Agathe. "I am the dove!"

The Hermit suddenly appeared under the tree where the dove sat. He waved his hand, and the bird flew to the tree where Caspar was hiding.

Max was following the bird's flight with his rifle. He fired. Agathe screamed and fell. At the same instant, Caspar came tumbling out of the tree.

The Hermit lifted Agathe and carried her to a grassy mound. A cry went up that the huntsman had killed his bride.

But Agathe was soon conscious again. She had not been harmed. It was Caspar who had received the bullet.

Out of the earth rose Samiel, visible only to Caspar.

"Is this how you keep your word to me? Then take your victim!" cried Caspar. "I curse you and heaven!" He died in convulsions, and Samiel sank into the earth.

The others were shocked at Caspar's last words. The prince ordered that the body be thrown into Wolf's Glen, and some of the men carried it away.

Kneeling before Prince Ottokar, Max confessed that through Caspar's influence he had been in league with the Evil One—that he had fired four "free" bullets.

The prince was indignant. This man was not worthy of Agathe's hand and must either go to prison or leave the country, he declared.

Max's friends tried to intercede for him. The prince silenced them.

The Hermit came forward. "Such punishment is too severe," he said. "Even a prince should not refuse to hear repentance."

Prince Ottokar listened respectfully.

"Since this young man was true and brave," said the Hermit, "give him a year of trial. Then, if he finds favor in your eyes, let him be rewarded with Agathe's hand."

Prince Ottokar granted this petition. Agathe and Max expressed their joy, and the others joined them in a prayer of gratitude and hope.

Norma

VINCENZO BELLINI *was already known for several successful operas when he composed* Norma. *The story was based on a French tragedy. The libretto was by Felice Romani.*

Norma *had its first performance at La Scala in Milan on December 26, 1831. It was not well received, but the company had faith in the work and performed it until its success was assured.*

ACT I

A PROCESSION of Druids had come through the night to their sacred grove. They were led by the high priest, Oroveso. It was their duty, he told them, to watch the heavens. At the first light of the new moon their religious rite would begin.

The others spoke reverently of his daughter, Norma, who was high priestess. Would she come, they asked, to cut the sacred mistletoe?

Yes, he answered, Norma would come.

They spoke of the hated Roman army that occupied the land and of their plot to drive the enemy from Gaul. "Norma will come. She will bless our wishes," they said, and they passed through the grove and into the forest beyond.

From among the trees came two figures. One was the Roman proconsul, Pollione, ruler of the conquered province. The other was his friend, Flavio.

"All is still now," said Pollione. "We can walk freely here."

"We risk death in this wood," said Flavio. "Norma warned us."

"The name you have spoken chills my heart," said Pollione.

"What are you saying?" said Flavio. "Norma is your beloved, the mother of your children."

But he no longer loved her, said Pollione. His new love was Adalgisa, a beautiful priestess in the temple of the Druids.

"And she loves you?" asked Flavio.

"I dare to hope so," answered Pollione, but he feared the jealous wrath of Norma if she knew his true feelings. He told Flavio of a dream he had had. He and Adalgisa were in Rome, kneeling in the temple of Venus. A thunderbolt struck the altar, and his loved one vanished. He heard the wailing of his children, and a voice rang out, "Thus Norma avenges the treachery of her lover!"

A gong sounded.

"Listen," said Flavio. "Norma is on her way."

In the forest the Druids were hailing the first light of the moon.

"Barbarians!" exclaimed Pollione. "Love is stronger than all your power. I defy the worst you can do!" And he and Flavio hurried away.

Oroveso returned, leading the procession of Druids. When they had assembled beneath the great oak Norma

appeared among them. In her hand was a golden sickle.
She ascended the stone at the foot of the tree and stood
looking about her with a commanding air.

She spoke, as one inspired, "Who cries for war at the
holy altar? In the pages of the mystic volume I read that
Rome will fall, but not by you. Through her own vices she
will perish. Peace, all!"

With her sickle she cut branches of the sacred mistletoe, which priestesses received and placed in baskets.
Then Norma offered a prayer to the moon, the pure goddess who reigned in heaven.

"When the god of wrath decrees the fall of Rome," she
said, "my summoning voice shall be heard in thunder."

"Let it be heard," said the others, "and the proconsul shall be first to fall."

"Yes, first to fall," said Norma, but she knew in her heart that if Pollione returned with the love he had once felt for her, she would defend him against the rest of the world.

She went away. The rest of the procession followed.

Out of the woods came the young priestess, Adalgisa. Tormented by her love for Pollione, she threw herself down before the altar and prayed to heaven for protection.

Pollione and Flavio came upon her there. Flavio tried to draw his friend away.

"Leave me," ordered Pollione, and Flavio reluctantly left the two alone.

Pollione approached the altar. "What do I see?" he asked. "Tears, love?"

"I was praying," said Adalgisa.

"To a cruel god," said Pollione. "My beautiful one, the god who should receive your prayers is love."

She started to leave.

"Where can you go," he asked, "that I cannot follow?"

"To the temple," she said, "where I have taken my vows."

"And our love?" he asked.

"I have forgotten it," she answered.

He pleaded with her not to leave him. He asked her to come away with him to Rome. Her resolution wavered. She confessed at last that she could not bear to be separated from him.

"Then you will come with me?—tomorrow at this hour?" he asked.

"I swear," she said.

ACT II

Norma entered a room of her dwelling, and her friend Clotilde led in the two children, who had been kept hidden from the world.

"Take them out of my sight," said Norma.

"What is this feeling that divides you from your children?" asked her friend.

Norma could not tell. She only knew that she both loved and hated them. She told Clotilde the news she had heard. Pollione had been recalled to Rome.

"Will you go with him?" asked Clotilde.

"He has not said so," answered Norma. "What if he should desert me and his children?"

"Can you think he would?" asked her friend.

Norma was not sure, but she was afraid.

Someone was coming toward the dwelling, and Clotilde took the children back into hiding. Norma saw that her visitor was Adalgisa. She greeted the girl warmly and invited her in.

Adalgisa had been weeping.

"Speak. What troubles you?" asked Norma.

Adalgisa hesitated, then answered, "Love! I struggled against it, but I could not resist. Now I have sworn to leave the temple, betray the altar, and forsake my country."

Norma pitied the girl. "So young for such sorrow," she said. "How did these feelings begin?"

"With a look and a sigh," said Adalgisa. "I saw in his face another heaven."

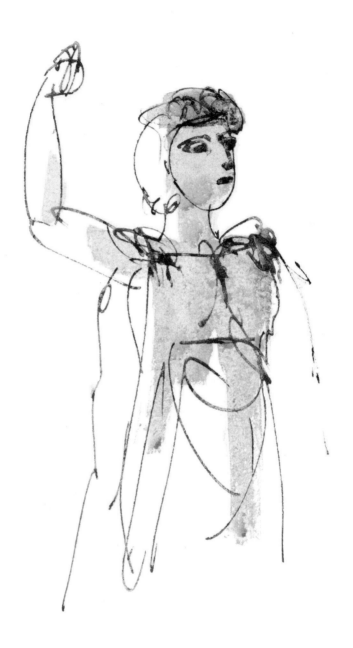

Norma recalled with grief that she had felt the same when she first met Pollione. She said gently, "You are not eternally bound to the altar. I pardon you and free you from your vows. Go, and be happy. But tell me—the man you love, which of us is he?"

"He was not born in Gaul," said Adalgisa. "Rome is his country."

"Rome?" said Norma. "Tell me his name!"

Adalgisa looked out the doorway at the man who was approaching. "You see him now," she said.

"He? Pollione?" cried Norma.

Adalgisa was bewildered. "Why are you angry?" she asked.

"Is that the man?" asked Norma. "Have I understood you?"

"Ah, yes," said Adalgisa.

Pollione entered. He started at the sight of Norma and Adalgisa together.

"You are trembling," said Norma fiercely. "For whom? Not for her. She is not guilty. Tremble for yourself and your children and me!"

Adalgisa waited for Pollione to defend himself, but he was silent.

"Oh, how you have been deceived!" said Norma in bitterness and rage. "It would have been better for you to die than ever to have known this man."

Pollione seized Adalgisa's arm and tried to lead her away.

"Leave me," she said. "You are unfaithful."

"No, I love only you," said Pollione desperately. "It is my fate to love you and leave her."

"Then go," said Norma, and she told the girl, "Go with him."

"I would rather die," said Adalgisa.

Again Norma tried to send Pollione away. "Forget me and your children," she said. "Forget your promises and honor. But you will find no peace. My hate will follow you."

"Hate me if you must. This love is stronger than you or I," declared Pollione.

But Adalgisa turned to Norma and said firmly, "Never again will I yield to my weakness. I would gladly die if I could only return this man to your children and to you."

A gong sounded, calling Norma to the temple. With one arm she repulsed Pollione. With the other she gestured imperiously for him to go, and he left the dwelling.

ACT III

Night had come. In Norma's bedroom the children were sleeping. Norma entered, carrying a lamp and a dagger.

The children must die, she told herself. In Gaul they were doomed to lives of shame and disgrace. In Rome they would be slaves.

She lifted the dagger, but she could not strike.

"Ah, no, they are my children!" she sobbed.

The children woke, and she held them in her arms. She called Clotilde and asked her to summon Adalgisa.

Adalgisa appeared.

"One thing I ask of you," said Norma. "I cannot take these poor children with me to the grave. I leave them in your care." She asked the girl to take them to their father in the Roman camp. "He may be a less faithless husband to you than to me," she said. "I forgive him, and now I die."

"A husband to me?" said Adalgisa. "Never!"

"I ask it for the children's sake," said Norma. "Take them with you. Protect them and never let them be abandoned to slavery. Remember, it was for you that I was cast aside."

"Then I will go to the ungrateful man," said Adalgisa, "and plead your cause until he returns to you."

Norma scornfully rejected the offer.

Adalgisa insisted that Pollione was sure to be repentant. "Let me either restore him to you," she said, "or let me hide myself with you forever, concealed from heaven and man."

Norma said at last, "You have won. I find a friend is left in you," and she and Adalgisa pledged eternal friendship to each other.

ACT IV

Warriors of Gaul had met near the Druids' wood. They spoke of Pollione, and they asked one another if he had left for Rome. Some of the men were sure he was still in camp.

Oroveso joined them, bringing the news that a more cruel commander had been sent to replace Pollione. New and powerful Roman legions had come with him.

"Does Norma know this?" asked the warriors. "Does she still counsel us to peace?"

"Her thoughts are hidden from me," said Oroveso. He advised the men to pretend submission until the time was right for them to rise against the Romans.

The warriors agreed to wait. "But woe be to Rome," they said, "when the signal to arms sounds from our sacred altar!"

Norma had come to the temple. She was calm now, confident that Adalgisa's mission would succeed. Pollione would return, a repentant lover, and the world would smile as in the first days of their happiness together.

Clotilde came running into the temple. "You must be brave!" she said. "Adalgisa's plea was in vain. She has come back to the cloister of the temple to offer up her vows."

"And he?" asked Norma.

"He swears he will come and carry her away," said Clotilde.

Norma's grief and rage overwhelmed her. She went to the altar and struck the sacred gong.

Warriors, priests, and priestesses came rushing in. Oroveso was among them. "The signal—what does it mean?" he asked.

"War and carnage!" answered Norma, and the Druids and warriors took up her cry.

Oroveso reminded her that the rite of war called for a human sacrifice. Who would be the victim?

She said grimly, "This altar has never lacked a victim." There was a tumult outside. "What is this?" she asked.

"A Roman has profaned our temple," Clotilde told her. "He was found in the cloister."

Warriors brought in the captured Roman.

"It is he!" said Norma.

"Pollione!" said Oroveso.

From her place at the altar Norma looked down in triumph.

"What led you here to violate our shrine?" asked Oroveso.

"Strike," said Pollione, "but do not question me."

"The blow shall be mine," said Norma. She took the sword from her father's hand and confronted Pollione. The Druids and warriors urged her to strike, but a strange weakness stayed her hand. On the pretext of wanting to question him further, she sent the others away.

When she and Pollione were alone she offered him a chance to save himself. "Swear that you will give up Adalgisa forever," she said. "If you promise this, I will grant you life and never see you again."

He refused.

In jealous fury she threatened that his children and the Roman conquerors would fall, that Adalgisa would die in flames.

"Take my life, but pity her," implored Pollione.

"At last you plead, but you are too late," she said. "You shall suffer as I have suffered."

She called back the Druids and warriors. "To your wrath I reveal a new victim," she said. "A priestess who has betrayed her holy vows."

"Again I implore you, have pity!" pleaded Pollione in anguish.

Norma hesitated. The thought came to her, "Shall I, so guilty, accuse another of my sin?"

All about her, voices were clamoring for the name of the guilty one.

"Do not tell them!" cried Pollione.

Norma spoke. "It is I," she said.

The others stared, unbelieving.

"You, Norma?" said her father.

"I, myself. Make the pyre ready," she said, and to Pollione, "In vain you tried to leave me. Fate brings us together in life and death."

"I have known you too late," he said. "Now you are lost to me, and with my remorse, I feel my love return."

The others were beseeching the priestess to take back her words.

This she could not do. She asked only mercy for her children.

Oroveso raised his voice to denounce her, but she saw his tears. "Ah, you forgive me," she said.

The Druids covered her with the black veil of death. The pyre was ready and burning, and Norma and Pollione walked together toward the flames.

The Flying Dutchman

RICHARD WAGNER *wrote* The Flying Dutchman— *both libretto and music—in 1841 while living near Paris. The story was based on an ancient legend. Wagner had written the opera for production in his native Germany, but it was refused by one German opera company after another. At last, on January 2, 1843,* The Flying Dutchman *was performed in Dresden. The audience found the music gloomy and strange, and it was many years before the opera was accepted as one of* Wagner's *great works.*

ACT I

A NORWEGIAN SHIP lay at anchor off the coast of Norway. A storm had driven her off-course, and the captain had gone ashore to survey the country and find out where they had landed.

While the sailors worked and sang on deck, Captain Daland stood on a rock and looked about him. He recognized the stretch of coast. They were in the bay of Sandwike, seven miles beyond his home.

He went back on board his ship. The storm was subsiding, the danger was past. The sailors went below to rest, and he followed them. Only the steersman was left on deck

to keep watch. He walked for a while, then sat down. He yawned, tried to rouse himself, and slowly went to sleep.

The sky darkened. The wind rose again, and out of the storm came another ship. Her sails were blood-red, her masts were black. Quickly she put into the bay. As her anchor went crashing overboard, the Norwegian steersman awoke. Without leaving his place, he glanced toward the wheel, then went back to sleep.

In silence the crew of the other vessel furled the sails. A pale, black-bearded figure went ashore. He was the Flying Dutchman, captain of the ghostly ship. In centuries past he had offended Satan, who had pronounced upon him a terrible doom. He must sail the seas forever, with a brief period on shore only once in seven years. His one hope of redemption lay in the love of a faithful woman, but over the years this hope had become a mockery.

Captain Daland came up from his cabin and saw the strange vessel. He wakened the steersman, who started up in confusion and began to hail the ship.

There was no answer.

Daland called to the man on shore, "Tell me your name and country."

"I have come far," answered the Dutchman. "Would you drive me away?"

"No, God forbid," said Daland. "I give you welcome. Who are you?"

"A Dutchman," said the other man.

Daland went ashore. The two men talked—Daland of his home nearby, the Dutchman of his lonely, ceaseless wanderings.

"What cargo do you carry?" asked Daland.

The Dutchman had a chest brought ashore—a chest filled with the rarest pearls and precious stones. "Will you bargain?" he asked.

Daland gazed in wonder. Who could buy such treasures? he asked. Who had wealth enough to offer the price?

"The price?" said the Dutchman. "All these I offer you in return for a night's shelter. This is but a small part of my cargo of treasure. But what good are riches when I have neither wife nor child and can never return to my native land?" He asked abruptly, "Have you a daughter?"

"I have," answered Daland.

"Let her be my wife!" said the Dutchman.

Daland was incredulous.

"Give me your daughter," said the Dutchman, "and all my treasure will be yours."

"You offer jewels," said Daland. "A faithful wife is a fairer jewel still."

"She shall be mine?" asked the Dutchman.

"As you are bountiful, you have a good and noble heart," said Daland. "I wish you were my son."

The Dutchman thanked him and asked, "Shall I see your daughter today?"

"The next good wind will take us home," said Daland. "You'll see her then, and if she pleases you—"

"She shall be mine!" and the Dutchman asked himself, "Will she be my angel? Through her will I find rest and peace?"

The storm had passed. Daland boarded his ship and set sail for home. The Dutchman prepared to follow.

ACT II

In Daland's home a group of maidens had gathered to talk and spin. Senta, Daland's daughter, sat with them. Her nurse, Mary, was busily spinning with the others, but Senta sat idle. She was lost in contemplating a picture on the wall—the portrait of a pale, black-clad man with a dark beard.

The maidens sang of their sweethearts who sailed in distant places and earned much gold. "The gold for her who duly spins," they sang. Mary chided Senta for her idleness. "Careless girl," she said, "you will win no gift from your sweetheart."

"She has no need to work as we," said the maidens. Senta's sweetheart did not go to sea. He was a hunter who brought her game instead of gold.

And yet, complained Mary, the girl was gazing at that picture and dreaming her life away.

The maidens said to one another, "She is sighing for that pale man." Erik, the hunter, was hot-tempered, they said. If he grew angry he might shoot his rival down from the wall!

Senta told them sharply to be quiet, and when their laughter and singing grew louder than ever, she cried out that their noise was tiring her ears.

"Then sing, yourself," they said, and they called for the Ballad of the Flying Dutchman.

She sang the song of the ghostly captain who roved the seas. The ballad told how he had sworn to sail around a cape through a raging storm. Satan, offended by the oath, had condemned him to roam forever. Only a faithful wife could redeem him from his curse.

"Ah, where is she who will be faithful?" asked the maidens.

Senta rose to her feet. She spoke, as if to the Dutchman, "I am the one who will save you. May God's angel guide you here!"

"Heaven help us!" cried Mary and the maidens.

Someone else spoke. "Senta, would you forsake me?" It was Erik, the hunter, who had just entered.

The maidens appealed to him for help. They feared the girl had gone mad. Mary blamed the picture and declared that it should be destroyed when Senta's father returned.

"He comes now," said Erik.

Senta had been standing in a trance. At Erik's words she seemed to waken. "My father comes?" she asked.

"From the height I saw his ship," said Erik.

The maidens would have run down to the landing, but Mary stopped them. They must have food and wine ready for the sailors, she said, and she drove them out of the room.

Senta started after them, but Erik kept her there.

"What's to become of me?" he said. "Before your father sails again, he will choose a husband for you." And since Erik could offer only a hunter's skill and a frugal hut, there was small chance that he could be chosen.

"Why must we speak of this now?" she said. "Let me go to welcome my father."

Erik asked if she would plead his cause to her father. "Why do you doubt me?" she said. "Why this suspicion?"

Daland cared only for gold, said Erik. Only someone with riches could hope to win her hand. This thought filled him with grief, and to add to the torture, she worshiped the picture on the wall and loved to sing the Ballad of the Flying Dutchman.

"Why should I not be moved by his sad story?" she asked.

"Surely you should have more sympathy for me," he said.

"What can your sorrow be!" she said. "Do you have the fate of this hapless man?" She drew him close to the picture. "Look, can you feel the pain in that face? My heart aches when I think of his suffering."

"May God protect you, you are in Satan's power!" said Erik. He told her of a dream he had had. In the dream he had seen two seamen. One was Senta's father. The other was a pale stranger dressed in black. Senta came to greet

them. She knelt before the stranger, who lifted her to his breast and kissed her, then carried her off to his ship.

Senta had been listening with eyes closed. "He seeks me! I must wait for him!" she cried.

"My dream was true!" exclaimed Erik, and he rushed away in despair.

Senta was gazing at the picture. "I pray that heaven may soon grant his prayer," she said.

Daland entered and, with him, the Dutchman. Senta's eyes turned from the pictured face to the face of the stranger. She stood spellbound. He moved slowly toward her.

Daland reproved Senta for having no word of greeting for her father. She welcomed him then. She asked, "Who is this stranger?"

He was a homeless wanderer, said Daland, who had gained great treasure in foreign lands. He said proudly to the Dutchman, "Did I not do well to sing her praises? Is she not beautiful?" He told his daughter, "Receive him kindly. You have only to command, and tomorrow he will be your bridegroom. Look at these jewels, these bracelets. They are nothing compared to the rest of his treasures, and all are yours when you are his."

Neither Senta nor the Dutchman gave any sign of having heard him. They were lost in gazing at each other. Puzzled, Daland withdrew.

Still Senta and the Dutchman stood motionless. To him she was the fulfillment of all his hopes. To her he was someone she had known and loved in her dreams.

He said at last, "Will you be mine forever? Shall I find peace and rest in your love?"

"Whoever you are, whatever the curse that is on you, I shall obey my father's will," she said.

They pledged their love to each other. He called out in defiance of fate, "Your power is laid low!" and she said tenderly, "Here may he have a home. Here may he rest."

Daland returned. It was the custom of his people to celebrate the end of a voyage with a feast, he said, and they were impatient to begin. He hoped that this might be a marriage feast. He asked his daughter if she consented to wed his friend.

Senta and the Dutchman joined hands.

"I will be faithful until death," she promised.

"My grief is ended," said the Dutchman.

Daland wished them happiness. "Now," he said, "we can go to the feast with joyful hearts."

ACT III

Night had come. In the rocky harbor near Daland's house the two ships lay at anchor. Daland's ship was brightly lighted, and sailors were singing and dancing on deck. The Dutchman's ship was dark, and the stillness of death hung over it.

The maidens brought baskets of food and wine down to the shore. Bypassing the Norwegian ship, they went toward the Dutch vessel.

"Stop! What are you doing?" shouted the Norwegian sailors.

"Do you think this is all for you?" returned the maidens. "Your neighbors, too, must have a share."

But when they called up to the Dutch ship, there was no answer.

"They are dead," said the Norwegian sailors, pretending great sorrow. "They have no need for food or drink."

The maidens continued to hail the Dutch ship.

"They are all down in the hold, watching over their treasure like dragons," said the Norwegian sailors.

"Have you no sweethearts on land? Will you not come and dance with us?" the maidens called to the Dutch ship.

"They are old and gray, and all their sweethearts are dead," said the Norwegian sailors.

The sight of the dark, ghostly-looking ship began to alarm the maidens. They turned back to the other vessel and handed the baskets up to the sailors.

The men invited the girls to come on board.

"Not just now. Later we may," said the maidens, and they went back to the house.

The men emptied the baskets. As they ate and drank, they grew more and more boisterous. Deliberately they tried to rouse the Dutch crew.

Waves rose about the other vessel. A storm-wind whistled through her rigging. A bluish flame flared up like a watch-fire on the ship, and life began to stir on board.

The Dutch sailors burst into song. Fiercely and mockingly they sang of their captain and his vain search for a faithful bride.

"What a song!" the Norwegian sailors said to one another. "Are they ghosts?"

The Dutch crew sang on. The storm grew wilder about the ship.

Horror gripped the Norwegian sailors. They left the deck,

making the sign of the cross as they went, and the shrill laughter of the Dutch crew followed them.

With magical suddenness the air and sea were calm again, and the Dutch ship was dark and silent as before.

Out of the house came Senta and Erik. He was angrily accusing. She was trying to escape from him, as he denounced her for her blind obedience to her father.

"I can see you or think of you no more," she said. "Higher calls are mine."

"What higher calls?" he asked. Was not her highest call to keep her promise to him—her promise of eternal love?

She was frightened. "What!" she exclaimed. "Did I promise you this?"

"Oh, Senta, do you deny it?" he asked sorrowfully, and he reminded her of a day when they had stood together, watching her father's ship leave the harbor. "With your arm about my neck, you pledged your love," he said. "With your head on my breast, you clasped my hand. Did that not tell me you were true?"

Without their knowing, the Dutchman had come upon them. He had been listening. "Lost!" he cried out. "All is lost forever!"

Shocked and amazed, they turned toward him.

"Senta, farewell," said the Dutchman, and he started away.

She begged him to stop.

"Back to the sea till the end of time," he said. "I can never be saved." He blew a note on his whistle, signaling his sailors. "Set the sails—up with the anchor!" he ordered them.

"Do not doubt me," pleaded Senta. "I have been faithful."

"You are under an evil spell," said Erik. "Come to me."

All the while, the Dutchman was accusing Senta of having made a cruel jest of his love. He told her of the curse that had been placed on him. Only a faithful woman could lift the curse, he said, and those who broke their vows to him were doomed to endless damnation. Yet he promised her that she would not be doomed. Because she had never pledged her love to him in the name of God, she would be saved.

"I know you well, and I know your fate," she answered. "My love shall take away the curse."

"Help, or she will be lost!" cried Erik.

Daland, Mary, and the maidens came out of the house. The Norwegian sailors gathered on land.

The Dutchman had already boarded his ship. The sails were set, and the vessel left shore. Senta tried to run down to the strand, but her father, Erik, and Mary held her back.

She freed herself and ran to the cliff overlooking the harbor. With all her strength she called after the Dutchman, "Here I stand, faithful unto death!" and she threw herself into the sea.

Immediately the Dutch ship sank. The waves rose high and subsided in a whirlpool. A light broke over the wreck of the ship. In the glow the figures of Senta and the Dutchman, in each other's arms, floated upward from the sea.

Simon Boccanegra

GIUSEPPE VERDI *had already composed some of his greatest operas—including* Rigoletto, Il Trovatore, *and* La Traviata—*when he wrote* Simon Boccanegra. *Francesco Piave furnished the libretto, which he based on a drama by the Spanish playwright, Antonio Gutiérrez.*

Simon Boccanegra *was first performed in Venice on March 12, 1857. It was a failure, partly because of a poor cast, partly because the complicated story was hard to follow. More than twenty years later Boïto, the poet and composer, rewrote the libretto, and Verdi rewrote most of the music. The new version was first given in Milan on March 24, 1881. The performance was a triumph.*

PROLOGUE

ON A SQUARE in Genoa two men had met to discuss a political plot. At that time, toward the middle of the fourteenth century, Genoa was a republic, torn by strife between commoners and nobles. The two men, Paolo and Pietro, hoped to have a commoner chosen as head of the state. Their candidate was Simon Boccanegra, a national hero, who was renowned for having driven back the African pirates.

Pietro left to stir up sentiment among the people. Simon

Boccanegra came out of the night, approached Paolo, and asked him, "Why have you sent for me?"

"Do you wish to be elected doge?" asked Paolo.

"I? No," said Simon.

"Are you not tempted by the crown?" asked Paolo.

"You are dreaming!" said Simon.

Paolo asked, "What of Maria?" and Simon questioned him eagerly for news of her. Paolo pointed to the Fiesco palace facing the square. Maria was a prisoner there, he said, and he suggested that as doge of Genoa, Simon might be united with the unhappy girl.

Paolo asked again if Simon would accept the crown. Thinking of his beloved Maria, Simon agreed.

People were approaching, and Simon left the square. Paolo stepped out of sight. Pietro appeared with a crowd of sailors and laborers. He was urging them to support a hero and commoner in the coming election.

"Who?" asked the people.

"Simon Boccanegra!" said Paolo, coming forward.

It was well known that the powerful Fiesco family and Simon were enemies. The crowd asked doubtfully what the Fiesco family might do if Simon should be elected.

"They will keep their peace," said Paolo. Pointing to the Fiesco palace, he told the crowd about the beautiful girl who was held prisoner there. The others knew of her. It was months since they had seen her face.

A strange light burned in the palace. Fearing that evil spirits were abroad, the men hurried away.

Fiesco came out of his palace, bowed with grief. Not only had he failed to protect his daughter from the world, but death had taken her from him.

Mourning women and men left the palace, crossed the square, and disappeared.

Simon returned. He was elated at having heard his name spoken on all sides. As ruler of Genoa, he thought, he could surely free Maria and claim her as his wife.

He saw Fiesco and asked his mercy and forgiveness.

"You are late," said Fiesco. "Even if you were to ascend the throne, my hate would follow you."

"Peace," said Simon.

"There can be no peace till one of us is dead," answered Fiesco.

"Will my blood end the strife?" asked Simon, and he bared his breast. "Then strike here."

The other man haughtily refused to strike, and he offered pardon on one condition. A child had been born to his daughter and Simon. "Give me this unfortunate child, whom I have never seen," said Fiesco. "I swear to live for her happiness, and you shall be forgiven."

Simon replied that it was not in his power to give up the child. She had disappeared. He had left her in the care of an old woman, who had died. The child had wandered away, and he had never found her.

"If you cannot grant my wish, there can never be peace between us," said Fiesco harshly, and he turned away.

Thinking of Maria, Simon was suddenly determined to see her. The palace door was unlocked, and he went inside. After a little while he made his way out onto the balcony. He had found the house dark and silent.

Beside the balcony was a shrine of the Madonna with a lamp burning beside it. He took the lamp to light his way and went back inside. His voice rose in an anguished cry, "Maria! Maria!"

Fiesco, listening outside, knew that Simon had found Maria's body, and he said grimly to himself, "The hour of your punishment has come!"

Simon staggered out of the palace. From a distance voices called his name. Crowds of people carrying torches gathered in the square. Paolo and Pietro were there. Jubilantly they told Simon, "The people acclaim you doge!"

"Paolo! Ah, a tomb—" began Simon.

"A throne!" interrupted Paolo.

In the shadow of the palace Fiesco had been listening. "Simon the doge?" he said. "Hell is in my breast!"

There was a clamor of bells and drums, while the crowd shouted, "Long live Simon, the people's chosen one!"

ACT I

In the garden of the Grimaldi palace near Genoa a beautiful young woman known as Amelia Grimaldi stood watching the sunrise.

Her lover, Gabriele Adorno, entered. He greeted her joyously, but anxiety clouded her happiness. She feared that he and other nobles were in danger because of their plot to overthrow Simon Boccanegra, who for the past twenty-five years had been doge of Genoa. She believed her guardian, Andrea, was also plotting against the doge.

As Gabriele tried to reassure her, a herald from Simon Boccanegra was announced.

The herald was Pietro, now one of Simon's courtiers. The doge was on his way home from a hunting trip, he said, and wished to stop for a while at the Grimaldi palace.

"He may come," said Amelia.

When Pietro was gone she told Gabriele the reason for Simon's visit. "He seeks my hand," she said. The doge wished her to marry his favorite courtier, Paolo.

She and Gabriele made hasty plans for their own marriage, so that they could be man and wife before the doge made his formal offer.

She went into the palace. Gabriele stayed behind and

spoke with her guardian, who had just come into the
garden. The young man told of his love for Amelia and
asked, "Do you consent to our marriage?"

"There is a secret surrounding the girl," said Andrea.
"When you know the truth, your love for her may end."

"I am not afraid," said Gabriele.

"She is of humble birth," said Andrea.

"Grimaldi's daughter?" said Gabriele in amazement.

Grimaldi's true daughter died in a convent in Pisa,
Andrea told him. Her place was taken by an orphan girl
found on the convent grounds.

"But how does she bear the Grimaldi name?" asked
Gabriele.

Andrea explained. The Grimaldi men had been exiled. The doge sought to confiscate their wealth, but the girl, whom the world believed to be the heiress, kept the treasure from him.

"I love the orphan," said Gabriele.

"And you are worthy of her," said Andrea. He gave his consent for the two to marry.

Trumpets sounded, announcing the doge. Gabriele and Andrea left the garden. Simon Boccanegra, Paolo, and a group of their followers entered.

Simon sent the others away. As Paolo left, he caught sight of Amelia, who had come to greet the doge. "What beauty!" he sighed.

Simon asked Amelia if her exiled brothers did not long for their homeland.

"Yes," she answered.

He handed her a paper—a pardon for the exiled Grimaldi men. "They owe my mercy to you," he said, and he asked her, "Why do you hide your beauty in this place?"

She was quite happy, she said. She loved a young nobleman who loved her. And before the doge could bring up the matter of her marriage to Paolo, she told him, "There is a greedy villain who pursues me in reaching for the Grimaldi gold."

"Paolo?" asked the doge.

"That is his name," said Amelia, "and since you show so much concern for me, I wish to tell you my secret. I am not a Grimaldi."

"Then who are you?" he asked.

She told her story. As a child, she had lived in a cottage near Pisa. She had a picture of the mother she had never known. It had been given to her by the old nurse who cared for her. She remembered the death of the nurse, and she recalled a seafaring man who had sometimes come to the cottage.

Simon had listened in growing excitement. "Was Giovanna the name of the nurse who tended you?" he asked.

"Yes," said Amelia.

"And the picture—was it like this?" he asked. He showed her the miniature he carried with him. From her bosom she took her mother's picture.

"They are the same!" she cried.

"You are my daughter!" he said, and he caught her in his arms.

He planned a world of happiness that they would share. She promised to be a faithful and loving daughter. He led her across the garden and looked after her blissfully as she disappeared into the palace.

Paolo returned. "What was her answer?" he asked.

"Give up every hope," said Simon.

"I cannot!" protested Paolo.

"It is my will," said Simon sternly, and he went into the palace.

Pietro joined his friend in the garden, and Paolo angrily told him what had happened.

"What will you do?" asked Pietro.

"Carry her off," said Paolo.

Together they planned to seize the girl and take her away to the home of Lorenzino, a local politician who could be blackmailed into helping them.

*

The doge was presiding at a meeting of his council. With him in the council chamber were twelve noble counselors, twelve commoners, and other court officials. Paolo and Pietro were seated among the commoners.

The meeting was interrupted by a riot in the square outside. A mob had attacked Gabriele Adorno, and another man had come to his aid.

People were shouting, "Death to the nobles! Long live the people!" Other voices raised the cry, "Death to the doge!"

Simon rose with dignity. "Death to the doge?" he repeated. "Well!" He sent a herald to open the palace doors and invite the mob inside.

The crowd burst into the council chamber, pushing Gabriele and Andrea ahead of them. It was Andrea who had come to Gabriele's aid.

Simon asked what had happened.

Gabriele answered defiantly, "I have killed Lorenzino. He had stolen Grimaldi's daughter."

"A lie!" shouted the mob.

"Before he died, the villain revealed that a man of power had urged him to the crime," said Gabriele.

Pietro whispered to Paolo, "You are discovered!"

The doge asked the name of this man of power.

"Never fear," said Gabriele. "Lorenzino died before he could speak it." He looked at the doge with such intentness that Simon asked, "What do you mean?"

"*You* are the man!" said Gabriele. He broke away from the people who held him and tried to attack the doge.

Amelia had just come to the doorway. She threw herself between them.

Guards dragged Gabriele back. Amelia pleaded for him.
"Spare his life."

Simon gave the order, "Let no one harm him," and he
asked Amelia to tell how she had been stolen away and
how she had escaped.

She was alone by the sea, she said, when three men seized
her and carried her off to the house of Lorenzino. Knowing
Lorenzino's cowardice, she threatened him, and he released her.

The listening crowd agreed that he had deserved death.

"There is another here who deserves worse," said Amelia,
and she looked toward Paolo.

Simon and Gabriele asked the name of the villain. The
commoners were sure he must be a noble. The nobles were
equally sure he was a commoner.

The two rival groups threatened one another. Simon
quieted them, and for the protection of Gabriele and Andrea, he decided to detain the two men in the palace that
night. He called Paolo before him and looked at the shrink-
ing courtier with cold suspicion.

"Within these walls is a scoundrel who hears my words and trembles," said the doge. "Before heaven and in my sight, you bear witness. May he be accursed! Repeat it after me!"

Paolo, trembling and horrified, repeated, "May he be accursed!" and all the others echoed the words.

ACT II

That night Paolo and Pietro were alone in the doge's quarters. Paolo sent Pietro to bring Gabriele and Andrea to him by way of a secret passage.

After his friend had gone, Paolo shuddered at the recollection of the curse he had pronounced on himself. Hating and fearing the doge, he determined to be revenged. On a table in the room were Simon's water carafe and goblet. Paolo poured a vial of poison into the goblet.

Pietro led Gabriele and Andrea into the room and left them with Paolo.

Paolo asked Andrea, "Was it you who incited the rebellion?"

"Yes," replied Andrea.

Paolo confessed that he, too, was the doge's enemy. Wishing to make doubly sure of Simon's death, he proposed that Andrea murder the doge. In return, Paolo promised to aid in the rebellion.

Andrea indignantly refused, and Paolo ordered him back to the dungeon.

Gabriele was left behind, and he denounced Paolo for his cowardly plot against the doge.

"Then you do not love Amelia?" said Paolo.

"What are you saying?" asked Gabriele.

Paolo answered craftily that Amelia was here in the palace—that the doge was now her lover. He went away then, hoping that when Simon came into the room, Gabriele would strike him down.

Gabriele was filled with rage and despair. His father had been murdered by the doge. Now a double crime rested on the head of the tyrant.

Amelia entered and was startled to find Gabriele there.

"And why are *you* here?" he asked. He spoke of the doge with loathing, and called him "the monstrous villain who loves you."

"With an honorable love," she said.

"And you?" he asked.

"I love him, too," she answered. There was a secret, she

informed him, that could not yet be revealed, and she begged him not to doubt her.

A trumpet call signaled that the doge would soon be there.

"He must not find you here," she warned Gabriele, and she led him to a hiding-place on the balcony.

Simon entered with a letter in his hand. The letter listed enemies of the doge. On the list, he told Amelia, was the name of Gabriele Adorno.

"Forgive him," she said.

"I cannot," said the doge.

"Then I shall die with him," she said.

He held out a hope to her. "If he repents, perhaps pardon—"

She tried to assure him that Gabriele would repent, and she went away, praying that she might find a way to save him.

Simon wearily wondered how to resolve the cares and problems of state. He poured water into the goblet, drank, and wryly observed that even clear water was bitter to the lips of one who ruled.

He sat down and closed his eyes. Soon he was asleep.

Gabriele came out of his hiding-place. He looked down on the sleeping doge, and for a while a kind of fear or reverence stayed his hand. Then, with resolution, he drew a dagger.

Amelia rushed in. "Madman!" she cried.

Simon woke and sprang to his feet. The two men faced each other.

"Who unlocked the door for you?" asked the doge.

"None shall ever know," said Gabriele.

Simon threatened him. "Through torture you will speak."
"I fear neither death nor torture," replied Gabriele.

"Ah, you have avenged your father all too well," said
Simon. "You have stolen my daughter from me."

Gabriele was stunned to learn that Amelia was Simon's
daughter. When he had recovered he asked her to forgive
his jealous rage. He humbled himself before the doge.

Amelia prayed that her father's heart might be moved
to pity, and at last Simon extended a hand to the young
nobleman.

Outside, enemies of Simon were in open rebellion. The
doge offered Gabriele the chance to go and join the ranks,
but the young man vowed never to fight against the father
of Amelia.

"Then take a message of peace to them," said Simon.

Gabriele promised that if his words did not disarm the
people, he would fight beside the doge.

"Amelia shall be your prize," said Simon.

ACT III

A battle had been fought. Through the doorways of the
ducal palace the city was visible, brilliantly lighted in celebration of the doge's victory.

Andrea was still in the palace, where he had been held
during the uprising. Now he was free to go.

Guards brought Paolo into the castle. Andrea saw him
and asked where he was going.

"To my execution," answered Paolo. He had joined the
rebels and been captured. Simon Boccanegra had con-

demned him to death. "But," he said with vindictive pleasure, "I have already given death to him."

"What do you mean?" asked Andrea

"Poison is taking away his life," Paolo told him.

In the adjoining chapel a wedding chant was being sung. "Do you hear it?" said Paolo. "Gabriele Adorno is wedded to the one I carried off."

"Amelia? *You* carried her off? Monster!" cried Andrea, drawing his sword.

The other man invited him to strike, but Andrea restrained himself, and the guards led Paolo off to his execution.

Andrea watched the doorway. When he saw the doge outside, he concealed himself and waited. Simon entered. With him were a captain and a trumpeter.

The captain called to the citizens, who were celebrating in the square before the palace. It was the wish of the doge, he said, that the torches be extinguished out of respect for the dead heroes.

He and the trumpeter went away. Simon remained, looking dazed and ill. He turned toward the harbor and felt a cooling breeze on his face. Wistfully he recalled the heroic days of his young manhood. "The sea!" he said. "Why did I not find a tomb in your arms?"

"It would have been best for you," said Andrea, coming out of hiding.

"Who dares to come here?" asked Simon.

"One who is not afraid of you," answered Andrea. The end had come for the conqueror, the sentence of death had been written, he said. As he spoke, the lights of the city and harbor slowly began to die.

Simon asked, "Whose voice do I hear?"

Andrea replied, "You have heard it before." He revealed his secret. Andrea was the name he had assumed for his protection, but once the doge had known him as Fiesco, Maria's father. Now, he said, he had come to claim his revenge.

"No," said Simon. "Through you, peace comes again."

"What is this?" asked Andrea.

"Once you offered me pardon if I gave you the child I had lost," said the doge. "Now I have found her—as Amelia Grimaldi."

Andrea was overcome by emotion. He began to weep.

The doge spoke of the new life they might enjoy in friendship.

"It is too late," Andrea told him. "A cowardly traitor has poisoned you."

And now the doge knew that the illness he felt was the approach of death.

Amelia and Gabriele entered with members of the wedding party. She was startled to find Andrea there. Simon said, "In him you see the father of Maria, who gave you life."

"Can this be true!" she cried. To her the reunion meant an ending to the years of fatal feuds. But to Simon it was the end of life. While Amelia and Gabriele knelt before him, he spoke his last words: "Let my crown fall to Gabriele Adorno."

Andrea went to the balcony and addressed the people, "Hail Gabriele Adorno, now your sovereign doge."

Crowds in the square called back, "No! Boccanegra!"

"He is dead," said Andrea. "Peace be upon his soul."

Un Ballo in Maschera

GIUSEPPE VERDI *composed* Un Ballo in Maschera (A Masked Ball) *to a libretto by Antonio Somma. Somma based his text on still another libretto,* Gustavus III, *by the French dramatist, Eugène Scribe.*

The first performance of Un Ballo in Maschera *was to have been in Naples in 1858, but the local political situation was unsettled, and government officials feared the opera might incite a revolution. They called for so many changes in the story that Verdi withdrew his opera and took it to Rome, where censorship problems were not so great. The main change demanded by the Roman authorities was that the setting be moved from Sweden to somewhere outside Europe. So, for the first performance, on February 17, 1859, the background was shifted to colonial New England, and it was many years before the original setting was restored.*

ACT I

DEPUTIES, officers, and gentlemen had gathered in the royal palace of Sweden to await their king, Richard. The monarch was revered by most of them, but among the group was a band of conspirators, headed by Samuel and Thomas, who hated Richard and plotted in secret against him.

Oscar, a young page, announced the king. Richard entered and graciously received the petitions offered by the deputies.

A masked ball had been planned, and Oscar gave Richard the invitation list. Looking over it, the king paused at one of the names. "Amelia!" he said to himself. It was the name of the woman he loved.

His friends watched affectionately, believing he was lost in thought as he pondered their needs. His enemies told one another, "This is not the time to carry out our plans."

Renato, the king's friend and aide, had been waiting in the doorway to speak with Richard. He came in, as Oscar conducted the other visitors out.

Again Richard said to himself, "Amelia!" Then, seeing his friend, "Her husband!"

"You seem unhappy," said Renato.

Richard replied that he was oppressed by a secret care.

"I know all," said Renato gravely, and Richard was alarmed until his friend told him, "There is a plot against you. Your life is threatened."

"Ah, is that all?" said Richard in relief, and he brushed Renato's anxiety aside.

Oscar ushered in a judge, who presented papers to be signed.

"What is this?" said Richard, looking at the papers. "A woman to be banished? Why?"

The woman was Ulrica, a Negro fortuneteller, said the judge. She was a witch, in league with evil.

Oscar defended the woman. The fortunes she told always came true, he said.

The king asked that all his visitors be summoned back

into the room, and when they had gathered, he told them of a plan he had that promised great sport. They would all disguise themselves, go to Ulrica's, and test her powers.

Awed townspeople waited and watched in the firelit cave of Ulrica, while the fortuneteller chanted strange incantations.

Richard entered, dressed as a fisherman.

Sylvan, a sailor, stepped forward. For years he had served the king faithfully without reward, he said, and he asked Ulrica what was in store for him. She studied his palm and told him he would soon have gold and rank.

A kindly and humorous impulse seized Richard. Quickly he wrote on a paper, which he slipped into Sylvan's pocket.

Reaching into his pocket for money with which to pay Ulrica, Sylvan found the paper. It was a commission signed by the king. The sailor was elated, and there was great excitement among the people in the cave.

A manservant entered through a secret door in the back of the cave. Richard recognized him as Amelia's servant. He listened and heard the man say to the fortuneteller, "My lady waits outside. She wishes to speak with you in private."

Ulrica asked the others to leave for a while, and they all left the cave except the king, who remained hidden in the shadows.

Amelia entered through the secret doorway.

"What troubles you?" asked Ulrica.

"A bitter care that love has caused," answered Amelia.

"And what do you seek?" asked Ulrica.

Amelia replied that she sought peace from her love for the king.

Richard, listening, was overjoyed by this proof that Amelia returned his love.

Ulrica told her that a potion brewed from a certain magic herb would bring forgetfulness. "But you must pick the herb yourself at midnight," she said. She described the place where the plant could be found—at the foot of the gallows in a field near the city.

Amelia determined to go that evening. Richard resolved to follow her, so that she should not be in the fearsome place alone.

She let herself out through the back of the cave. Ulrica opened the main door. Samuel, Thomas, and their friends came in, along with Oscar, noblemen, and soldiers. They were all in bizarre disguises.

"Where is the king?" asked Oscar, and Richard whispered to him, "Quiet. No one must know who I am." He turned to Ulrica and in good-natured mockery questioned her powers.

She solemnly warned him not to laugh at fate. Examining his palm, she told him that he was a great ruler. Then she let his hand fall, saying, "Wretched man—go! Ask me no more!"

He pressed her to tell him what she had seen.

She told him at last that he was doomed to die by the hand of a friend.

Richard laughed at her prediction.

Ulrica gazed at Samuel and Thomas. "*You* do not laugh," she said. "What are you thinking?"

The two men said to each other, "Through her magic she knows all!" and Oscar and the others fearfully considered Ulrica's prophecy.

Richard asked who the assassin would be.

Ulrica answered, "The first person who shakes your hand today."

"Which one of you will prove the prediction false?" asked Richard, and he offered his hand to each of his companions. In superstitious fear, they refused to touch it.

Renato entered the cave. Richard ran to him and grasped his hand.

"This man whose hand I hold is my dearest friend," he said to Ulrica, and he revealed himself as the king. He threw her a purse and advised her to flee before she was exiled.

She thanked him for his generosity and tried to warn him of traitors close to him, but he ordered her to say no more.

Sylvan, with fellow sailors and townspeople, came to the door with words of praise for the king. Oscar, too, praised Richard. The king rejoiced in the loyalty of his subjects, but Renato recalled that ill-fortune often attended the greatest triumph. Samuel, Thomas, and their henchmen told one another that their vengeance was delayed by the flattering multitude. "He does not believe in fate," said Ulrica somberly, "yet he soon must die."

ACT II

Gallows field lay at the foot of a hill just outside the city. In the hour before midnight Amelia appeared on the hillside. She knelt to pray before continuing her way toward the spot where she hoped to find the magic herb.

A bell chimed midnight. A head seemed to rise out of the earth in her path—a terrible head with glaring eyes. She fell to her knees, praying for strength.

Suddenly Richard was beside her. She cried out. She begged him to leave her.

"I can never leave you," he said.

But she belonged to someone else, she reminded him. She was the wife of his dearest friend.

He was conscious of everything that kept them apart, he told her, yet he could not deny his feelings for her.

She confessed that she loved him in return. He was exultant, but she foresaw only sorrow in such a love.

Footsteps sounded. Someone was coming toward them. "Renato!" exclaimed Richard.

"My husband!" said Amelia, terrified. She lowered her veil to conceal her face.

Renato spoke urgently. Assassins were waiting nearby. He had slipped through their ambush and come to warn his friend. He threw his cloak about Richard as a partial disguise and showed him a path by which he might escape.

The king took Amelia's hand, refusing to leave her.

Renato asked her, "Lady, can you not persuade him to save himself?" He moved away to see if the assassins were in sight.

Amelia told Richard that he must escape. "Go," she commanded him, "or I'll lift the veil from my face!"

"What are you saying!" he said.

She told him firmly, "Decide!"

Renato returned. The king appealed to him for help. "Promise me that you will escort the lady back to the city without lifting her veil."

"I promise," said Renato.

"And when you reach the city gate," said Richard, "you will leave her and go in the opposite direction."

"It shall be done," said Renato. Again he moved away to look for the conspirators.

Richard told himself miserably, "If I were not to blame, I should stay and challenge them. Now, guilty of love, I must run away."

"Go quickly," said Amelia.

Renato, coming back, echoed her words, and Richard hurried down the path.

From the heights came Samuel, Thomas, and their followers. Renato challenged them.

"It is not the king!" said the men.

They recognized Renato.

"We have not been as fortunate as you," said Samuel. "No beautiful woman is here to meet us."

Thomas demanded a look at the lady's face. Some of the men came close, peering at her in the light of their torches.

"Don't come any nearer," said Renato, with his hand on his sword.

"Are you threatening us?" asked Thomas scornfully, and he caught hold of Amelia's veil. Renato drew his sword. All the other men attacked him.

To save his life, Amelia intervened. She let her veil fall.

Renato was incredulous. The conspirators were hardly less surprised. "His wife!" they said, and they began to laugh at what they took to be the ludicrous picture of the lovesick husband stealing out into the moonlight to meet his wife!

Renato gazed down the path Richard had taken. He had saved the king, and this was his reward—shame, dishonor, and faithlessness.

Amelia was asking herself, "Where can I turn now? Where can I find compassion?"

Renato spoke in a low voice to Samuel and Thomas, "May I see you in my home tomorrow morning?"

Samuel asked the reason.

"Come, and you shall know," said Renato.

Samuel and Thomas and their followers started away. Renato and Amelia were left alone. "I promised to escort you to the city gate," he said.

She said to herself, "His voice strikes my heart like the knell of death."

And from the distance came the laughter of the conspirators.

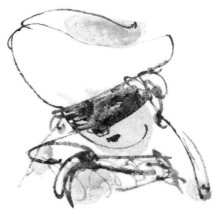

ACT III

It was morning. Amelia and Renato entered the study of their home. He put down his sword and closed the door. "For such an outrage there can be no excuse," he said. "You shall die."

She begged for mercy.

"You shall die," he repeated.

"It is true that for a moment I loved him," she said, "but God knows I did not dishonor your name."

He took up the sword. She realized that appeal was useless. She asked a final favor. "Let me say good-by to our son."

Without looking at her, he pointed to the door. "There is your son," he said, and she went out into the next room.

Realization came to Renato that it was not she who was most to blame. He looked at the large portrait of Richard on the wall. "It was you," he said. "You inspired my trust, then betrayed me. Now my heart holds only hate and death."

Samuel and Thomas arrived to keep their appointment.

Renato said bluntly, "I know your plans. You are going to kill Richard."

"And now you will betray us?" said Samuel.

"No," said Renato. "I wish to join you."

At first the conspirators mistrusted him. As a pledge, he offered the life of his son. "Kill him if I betray you."

With no more hesitation, Samuel and Thomas accepted
his offer. The three decided to draw lots to determine which
of them should kill Richard. Samuel wrote their names on
three slips of paper and dropped them into a vase.

Amelia returned. "Oscar is here," she said, "with an invitation from the king."

"Let him wait," said Renato. He told her to draw a name
from the vase.

"Why?" she asked.

"Ask no questions," he said, but she half-guessed the
purpose of the lottery, and her hand shook as she drew a
name.

Samuel looked at the slip of paper. "Renato," he said.

Renato exulted at his good fortune, and now Amelia was sure he sought the king's death.

Oscar entered and delivered an invitation to a masked ball to be held that evening.

"Will the king be there?" asked Renato.

"Certainly," answered Oscar.

Renato exchanged glances with Samuel and Thomas, and he accepted the invitation for himself and his wife. Samuel and Thomas decided that they, too, would be present.

Oscar described the ball—how brilliant, how splendid it would be. Amelia reminded herself miserably that it was she who had drawn the fatal slip of paper. Renato, Samuel, and Thomas pictured their enemy struck down in the midst of the evening's festivities. Speaking softly to one another, they agreed to wear blue dominoes with red sashes, and their password would be "death."

All the while, Amelia was casting about for a way to warn Richard without betraying her husband.

Shortly before the ball was to begin the king sat alone in his study. He had reached a decision. A sense of honor must separate him and Amelia forever.

He wrote an order that would send Renato to foreign duty. Amelia would go with her husband. She and the king would part with no farewells.

He signed the order and placed it inside his coat.

Sounds of dance music came from the ballroom. Amelia was there, he knew. He could see her if he chose, he could speak to her again. "But no," he told himself. Too much had come between them.

Oscar brought him a letter from an unknown lady.

Richard read the message—a warning that someone would attempt to assassinate him during the ball. "But if I stay away," he said to himself, "I shall be thought a coward." He told Oscar, "Get ready. We shall go together."

And after the page had gone, Richard exclaimed, "I shall see you again, Amelia. Once more I shall look upon your beauty!"

The ball had begun. Most of the guests wore masks. Samuel and Thomas and their followers were there, in blue dominoes and red sashes. Renato entered, wearing a similar costume. Samuel went close to him and spoke the password, "Death!"

"Death!" returned Renato. "But he will not be here." Word had come to him that the king would not appear at the ball.

A masked man was watching them, and the conspirators separated. Renato tried to lose himself in the crowd. The man followed. "You can't hide from me," he said mischievously. "You are Renato."

"And you are Oscar," said Renato, pulling off the page's mask. "Do you think it is right for you to come to the ball while your master is asleep?"

"The king is here," said Oscar.

Renato started. "Where?"

Oscar laughingly refused to tell. Renato pursued him about the dance floor, insisting that he must find the king and talk with him on an important matter. The page revealed at last that Richard was wearing a black cape with a pink ribbon on his chest.

Richard came forward. Amelia, in disguise, spoke to him. "Why have you come here? Go away."

"Was it you who sent the letter?" he asked.

Without answering, she pleaded with him to go. He recognized her. Under cover of the music they bade each other farewell.

Renato had drawn near. He thrust himself between them and stabbed Richard.

Amelia screamed. Oscar ran to Richard's side. Guests surrounded Renato and tore off his mask, crying, "Death to the traitor!"

"No, no!" said Richard. He took from his bosom the document that ordered Renato to a foreign post. He told Renato, "You and your wife were to go away together. I loved her, but I would not have brought dishonor to your name."

Amelia and Oscar wept. Renato was stricken with remorse.

"I am still your ruler," said Richard, "and I grant pardon to all." Dying, he took leave of those about him, and the people spoke in hushed voices, "Night of horror, night of horror!"

La Forza del Destino

GIUSEPPE VERDI *composed* La Forza del Destino (The Force of Destiny) *to a libretto by Francesco Piave. The text was based on a play by the Spanish dramatist Don Ángel de Saavedra, Duke of Rivas. The Imperial Italian Theater in St. Petersburg commissioned the opera and first performed it on November 10, 1862.*

ACT I

IN A ROOM of his castle near Seville the Marquis of Calatrava was saying good night to his daughter Leonora. He noticed that the balcony window had been left open, and he closed it. Looking into Leonora's sad face, he asked why she was so unhappy. "You have given up the stranger who was unworthy of you," he said. "Leave your future in my care."

As soon as he was gone, Leonora's maid, Curra, opened the window again and began to pack a traveling bag.

Leonora was weeping. She had deceived her father. She had not given up her lover, Don Alvaro, but had promised to elope with him that night, and her father's words were like daggers plunged into her heart. If he had stayed longer, she said, she might have told him the truth.

"Then tomorrow Don Alvaro would be dead or in

prison," said Curra, "and all because he loves someone who does not love him."

Leonora insisted that she did love him. Had she not promised to go with him, forsaking her father, home, and country?

Midnight struck. Don Alvaro was outside. He entered through the balcony window. There were swift horses below, he said, and a priest was waiting.

Leonora hesitated. "We will go tomorrow. I must see my father one more time," she said.

Don Alvaro began to doubt her love for him, and he offered to release her from her promise.

With new resolution she vowed that she would follow him forever.

There were footsteps on the stairs. The marquis burst into the room, followed by servants. In rage, he denounced his daughter and Don Alvaro.

Leonora tried to kneel before him.

"I am no longer your father!" he said, repulsing her.

"I alone am guilty," said Don Alvaro. "Strike me, and be avenged."

"Seize the villain," the marquis ordered his servants.

Don Alvaro drew his pistol, holding them back. "I yield to you alone," he said to the marquis. "Strike."

"So worthless a life should be ended by the hangman!" said the marquis.

"Your daughter is innocent," said Don Alvaro. "Let any doubt be ended with my life. Here I stand unarmed."

He threw away his pistol, which accidentally discharged as it struck the floor. The bullet wounded the marquis. "I am dying!" he cried.

Leonora ran to his side.

"Stay away," he ordered her. "The sight of you contaminates me."

His dying words were a curse, as he fell into the arms of his servants. They carried him away. Don Alvaro ran toward the balcony, dragging Leonora after him.

ACT II

The host and hostess were preparing supper in the kitchen of their inn. Several couples were dancing. Mule drivers were sitting about the room. Before the fire was the alcalde, a leading official of the village, and near the dining table sat a young man who had introduced himself as a student.

At one side of the kitchen a stairway led to a bedroom. While the hostess was serving supper, Leonora stepped out of the room above. She was disguised in men's clothing. Looking down into the kitchen, she saw the man who posed as a student. In terror, she recognized him as her brother, Don Carlo, who had sworn vengeance on her and Don Alvaro.

A gypsy girl, Preziosilla, came dancing in. "Long live war!" was her greeting, and she advised the men to seek their fortunes by going soldiering in Italy where war had broken out against the Germans.

The pretended student asked her to tell his fortune. She looked at his hand and told him he would suffer the greatest misery. "You are no student," she added. "I'll say nothing, but you haven't deceived me."

Pilgrims passed slowly by the inn. The group about the table stopped talking and singing long enough to pray with them, and Leonora prayed, "Save me from my brother."

Don Carlo began to joke about the little beardless person in men's clothing who had arrived with Trabuco, a mule driver. "Was it man or woman?" he asked.

"I notice nothing about travelers except their money," answered Trabuco.

Don Carlo kept asking about the little person, until Trabuco grew annoyed and left the table.

The alcalde said to Don Carlo, "You had better tell us who *you* are, where you are from, and where you are going."

"You wish to know?" asked Don Carlo, and he launched into a jumble of half-truths. He had been traveling with his friend, a nobleman, he said. Together they had been pursuing the assassin of his friend's father. The assassin had run away with the nobleman's sister. There were rumors that the girl had died and the murderer had sailed for America. The nobleman had left for the New World to hunt him down. "Now," he finished, "I am a student once more."

The others had listened with great seriousness, all except Preziosilla, who said skeptically, "Such stories carry no weight with me."

By that time supper was over. Bidding one another good night, they all left the kitchen.

Fearing for her life, Leonora had stolen away from the inn. Now, late at night, she came to the church of the Madonna of the Angels in the mountains near the village.

On the night of her father's death she and Don Alvaro had become separated. She had thought that he, too, was dead, but after overhearing her brother's story, she believed that Don Alvaro had deserted her and gone away to America, home of his Inca ancestors.

She prayed that her sin would be forgiven. Organ music and the monks' chanting came from within the church and mingled with her prayer.

She rang the bell outside the doorway to the monastery. Fra Melitone looked out through the grating in the door and shone a lantern in her face.

"Father Cleto has sent me," she said.

He invited her to come inside.

"I cannot," she said.

He called the superior, Father Guardiano. Leonora spoke with the superior alone. She explained why she could not enter the monastery. "I am a woman," she said. "Did not Father Cleto write to you?"

"He sent you?" said Father Guardiano. "Then you must be Leonora di Vargas."

"You shudder!" she said.

"No," he said. "Come in trust to the cross, and heaven will bless you."

There was a cross outside the monastery. She knelt before it. When she turned back to Father Guardiano she was able to speak calmly. Father Cleto had told her of a cell in the rocks nearby where a woman had once lived. Leonora wished to live there and devote her life to God.

He tried to persuade her to go to a holy cloister instead, but she insisted that her haven was here.

At last he gave her permission to live in the rocky cell, he alone to know her identity. Together they entered the porter's lodge.

Monks filed slowly into the church. They were followed by Father Guardiano and Leonora, who was disguised in a monk's habit. She knelt before him.

"A soul comes here to atone for his sins," said Father Guardiano. "The holy cave shall be opened to him. None of you shall pass the enclosure that surrounds it."

He told Leonora to rise and depart.

From this time on, no living creature should come to see Leonora, except when danger threatened or her last hour was at hand. Then she might ring the cave bell to summon aid.

Leonora and the monks prayed to the Virgin of the Angels. She rose and set out alone, and Father Guardiano extended his arms in blessing.

ACT III

Night had fallen along the battle front in Italy. Out of the woods came Don Alvaro, a captain of the Royal Spanish Grenadiers.

He believed Leonora dead, and he longed to die, too. While he meditated on his unhappy fate, he was startled by a cry for help. He ran into the woods to the rescue. There was a clash of swords, and he returned, leading a soldier—Don Carlo.

Carlo explained that he had been gambling, there had been a quarrel, and some of the other soldiers had attacked him. "Without your help, I should be dead," he said.

It was the men's first meeting, and they introduced themselves. Both had enlisted in the army under assumed names.

Carlo called himself Felice de Bornos. Alvaro gave his name as Federico Herreros.

An immediate friendship sprang up between them.

Shouts rose from the direction of the battle front, "To arms! To arms!"

"I'll go with you," said Carlo, and he and Alvaro left together.

By morning the fighting was still fierce. A doctor and several orderlies came into a receiving room in Spanish headquarters and posted themselves at windows where they could watch the battle.

"Herreros is leading the charge," said the orderlies.

"He has fallen!" said the doctor.

But the Germans were in retreat. Men were shouting, "Glory to Spain! Long live Italy!"

Alvaro was carried in, wounded and unconscious. Carlo was with him.

"Is there any danger?" he asked.

"There is a bullet in his chest," said the doctor.

Alvaro regained consciousness. "Let me die," he said.

"We will save you," said Carlo, "and you will be honored with the Order of Calatrava."

"Calatrava!" exclaimed Alvaro, wincing to hear the name of Leonora's father. "No, no!"

Carlo was puzzled, wondering why the name should have disturbed his friend.

Alvaro asked for a word alone with Carlo, and he said, when the others had gone, "In this solemn hour give me your word to do as I ask."

Carlo gave his word.

"Look in my bosom," said Don Alvaro.

Carlo looked and found the key to the box that Alvaro carried with him.

"Take from the box a packet. It contains a secret that must die with me," said Alvaro. "Promise to burn it."

Carlo swore that it should be done.

"Now I die in peace," said Alvaro.

The doctor and orderlies returned and carried Alvaro away.

A strange man, the gallant captain, thought Carlo. Why had he shuddered at the name of Calatrava? A suspicion came to him. What if this man should be his long-sought enemy?

The key was in his hand. Impulsively he opened the box and took out the packet. He paused, remembering his oath.

There was a small, unsealed case in the box. Regarding this he had made no promise. He opened the case. Inside was a portrait of Leonora.

Now he was sure. The wounded man was Alvaro.

The doctor looked in from the next room. "Good news," he said. "The man will live."

Carlo was filled with savage joy. Revenge was within his reach.

Just before dawn a party of soldiers on patrol duty cautiously investigated a military encampment. All was quiet, and they went their way. Alvaro entered the camp. Carlo came upon him there.

"Have you completely recovered from your wound?" asked Carlo.

Alvaro replied that he was quite well.

"Could you fight a duel?" asked Carlo.

"With whom?" asked Alvaro.

"Have you not received a message—Don Alvaro, the Indian?" said Carlo.

"Betrayer!" cried Alvaro. "So your promise was broken!"

Carlo denied that he had broken his word; he had looked only at the picture, he said. He revealed his true name: "I am Don Carlo di Vargas. And now one of us must die."

Alvaro answered that he could not fight a man to whom he had sworn eternal friendship. "It was destiny that killed your father," he said. "He and Leonora look down from heaven and tell you I am innocent."

Leonora was not dead, said Carlo. "An old relative gave her shelter, but by the time I arrived, she was gone."

"Then she lives!" said Alvaro, and he proposed that they search for her together.

"Fool!" said Carlo. "I must kill you, and after you, my shameless sister."

"Then you shall die first!" said Alvaro.

They drew swords and began to fight furiously.

The patrol came running to the scene and separated them. As he was taken away, Carlo shouted threats and insults.

"Now what is left to me?" Alvaro asked himself. "Merciful God, inspire my thoughts."

He threw down his sword. A longing had come to him for a life of forgetfulness and peace in some holy order.

He left the encampment.

The sun was rising, reveille sounded, and soldiers, women, and boys began to crowd the camp. Preziosilla, the gypsy, was there, busily reading palms. Trabuco, who had been a mule driver in Spain, had come to follow the army in Italy and was buying and selling merchandise in the camp.

Women and soldiers began a frenzied dance. Fra Melitone entered and was caught up in the dancing. When he had freed himself he announced that he had come from Spain to heal wounds and save souls, and he harangued the people for their sins.

The soldiers tried to drive him off. Preziosilla defended him. To draw attention from him, she seized a drum and began to play it. She sang, the others joined in, and the song rose to a pitch of patriotic fervor.

ACT IV

Beggars swarmed in the courtyard inside the monastery of the Madonna of the Angels. They had brought their bowls and were waiting to be fed. Father Guardiano was there, and in a little while Fra Melitone and another monk entered carrying a huge cauldron of soup.

The beggars pushed forward. Melitone ladled out the soup, all the time scolding them for their greed and ingratitude.

"Father Raphael treated us more kindly," said some of the women.

This angered Melitone so that he kicked the cauldron over and drove the beggars out.

Guardiano reproved him, "Be humble when you find that people prefer Raphael to you."

While they discussed Raphael, the gate bell rang. Guardiano left the courtyard. Melitone opened the gate and admitted Don Carlo.

Carlo haughtily asked for Father Raphael. Melitone went to find him.

For five years, ever since they were separated in Italy, Carlo had followed the trail of his enemy. The search had led him to this monastery, where he had heard that Alvaro was a monk known as Father Raphael.

Alvaro entered. The two men faced each other.

"You shall be punished by my hand," said Carlo. "Since you are a monk and have no weapons here, I have brought two." He offered Alvaro a choice of swords.

Alvaro asked him to go in peace.

"Neither this hermitage nor your garb can protect you, coward!" said Carlo.

Alvaro was stung by the insult, but he restrained himself. He asked for mercy and forgiveness.

"You left me a sister, abandoned and dishonored," said Carlo.

"She was not dishonored," said Alvaro. "I adored her. I love her now, and if she loves me, I could ask for nothing more."

"I'll not be placated by cowardly lies," said Carlo. "Take the weapon!"

Alvaro knelt at Carlo's feet, as no other man had ever seen him do.

"This act proves the stain on your birth," said Carlo, and he spoke tauntingly of the other man's mulatto blood.

Infuriated, Alvaro sprang up and snatched one of the swords from Carlo. Then, once more restraining himself, he threw down the weapon. "No, no!" he said. "Leave me."

Carlo slapped him across the face.

"Ah, you have decided your fate!" said Alvaro. He picked up the sword, and the two men rushed out of the courtyard.

Leonora came slowly out of her rocky cave. The years she had spent there had not eased her suffering. Alvaro was still in her thoughts, and she prayed to God for the peace that only death could bring.

From among the rocks she took up the bread that Guardiano had placed there for her. Then, hearing sounds of violence, she went quickly into her cave.

From a distance came Carlo's voice, "I am dying." He begged for absolution.

Alvaro came out into the space in front of the cave. He had lost his soul's salvation and could not give absolution to the man he had mortally wounded, but he knew of the holy hermit nearby who might perform the last rites.

He rang the cave bell.

Leonora opened the door. "Rash man," she said, "beware the wrath of heaven."

At the sight of her and the sound of her voice, he cried out, "No! It is a ghost!"

She recognized him. She said in wonder, "Once more I see you!" She came toward him.

He warned her to keep away. "There is blood on my hands." He pointed. "A dying man lies there."

"You have killed him?" she asked.

"I tried to avoid a fight," said Alvaro. "He found me here, insulted me."

She asked, "Who was he?"

"Your brother," he said.

Leonora ran into the woods where the dying man lay. In a little while she was brought back, supported by Guardiano. She was wounded.

"He would not forgive me before he died," she said brokenly. "To avenge himself, he has killed me."

Alvaro lifted his voice against this cruel vengeance of heaven.

"Do not curse," Guardiano admonished him. "Humble yourself to God."

"Yes, weep and pray," said Leonora. She spoke Alvaro's name as she died.

"Dead!" he sobbed.

"With God in heaven," said Guardiano.

Don Carlos

GIUSEPPE VERDI *composed* Don Carlos *on a commission from the Paris Opéra. The story was based on a play by Schiller, whom Verdi greatly admired. The libretto was begun by Joseph Méry and finished by Camille du Locle, after the death of Méry.*

Don Carlos *had its first performance in Paris on March 11, 1867, and was not an immediate success. Verdi rewrote the score in 1884, shortening it from five acts to four. Three years later he revised the work again and restored Act I, although the first act is sometimes omitted in performance.*

ACT I

ELIZABETH DE VALOIS, daughter of the French king, Henry II, had come with a hunting party to the forest of Fontainebleau. The group paused in a clearing where woodcutters were at work and their womenfolk sat about a fire. The princess went to them and threw them a few coins. Hidden among the trees, a young man stood watching her.

She and her party continued the hunt. Evening had come, and the woodcutters and their women set out for home. The young man was left alone. He was Don Carlos, crown prince of Spain. By royal decree he had been betrothed to the French princess, although they had never

met. Now that he had seen her, he was enchanted by her
loveliness. The light was fading. He was not sure he could
find his way out of the dark woods.

Elizabeth and her page, Thibault, returned. They had
become separated from the others and were lost. Don Carlos bowed to the princess and introduced himself as a
foreigner—a Spaniard.

"Do you belong with the company of Lerma, the Spanish ambassador?" she asked.

"Yes," he answered.

Thibault had seen the lights of Fontainebleau, and he
started toward the palace to bring back an escort for the
princess.

Elizabeth seated herself on a boulder. Don Carlos sat at
her feet, breaking up twigs and throwing them into the fire.
She spoke of the peace treaty between France and Spain
that might be signed tonight. He spoke of the coming marriage of Elizabeth and Don Carlos that was to be announced the next day.

She asked about the Spanish prince, wondering if his
love equaled hers.

"Don Carlos will live only to love you," he assured her.

"Why does my heart beat so? Heavens!" she exclaimed.
"Who are you?"

"The prince's messenger, I give you this," he said, hand-
ing her a small case containing his portrait. "He sends you
his likeness so you will know him."

She looked at the picture.

"I am Carlos," he said, "and I love you."

In her heart she had been afraid. Now she was ecstatically happy.

A cannon shot sounded—the signal that the peace treaty had been signed. Lights blazed up beyond the forest, illuminating the royal palace.

Don Carlos took Elizabeth in his arms, and they promised to love each other always.

Thibault returned. He kissed the hem of Elizabeth's skirt, telling her he brought glad tidings from the palace. "I greet you, your majesty, wife of King Philip!"

"No, no!" she said. "I am betrothed to his son."

But Thibault insisted, "You are queen."

Pages arrived with a litter for bearing the princess back to the palace. The Countess d'Aremberg, ladies-in-waiting, and other attendants came to accompany her. There was rejoicing among them that the war had ended and the princess would soon give her hand to King Philip of Spain.

Elizabeth and Don Carlos told each other despairingly, "All is over. The fatal hour has struck."

Count di Lerma, the Spanish ambassador, had come from the palace. He told Elizabeth that her father favored the marriage as a seal of friendship between the two nations. "But," he said, "King Philip wishes to leave you free to choose."

The group from the palace pressed her to accept. Count di Lerma asked, "What do you answer?"

The princess, knowing the decision had already been made, whispered, "Yes."

The count helped Elizabeth into the litter. The cavalcade moved away.

Grief-stricken, Don Carlos stood repeating the words, "The fatal hour has struck!"

ACT II

In Spain once more, the prince wandered in the cloisters of the Monastery of St. Just. Monks and an old friar were praying before the tomb of Emperor Charles V, Don Carlos' grandfather.

A bell tolled. The monks filed out. The old friar lingered and spoke to the prince, "The world's strife still haunts us here. Only in heaven will the spirit find peace."

Slowly and gravely he retired.

Don Carlos looked after him, feeling a chill of fear. Rumors persisted that the emperor's ghost stalked the cloister. For a moment it had seemed to him that the friar's voice was the emperor's voice—that beneath the friar's

habit he had seen the mantle and the crown of Charles V.

The prince's friend, Rodrigo, Marquis of Posa, joined Don Carlos in the cloister.

"The people of Flanders are calling you," said the marquis. "You must go and be their savior. But what is this?" he asked, noticing the prince's look of sadness.

Don Carlos revealed his secret—that he loved Elizabeth, who was now married to his father.

Rodrigo asked anxiously, "Has the king discovered this?"

"No," said Don Carlos.

"Then," said Rodrigo, "ask his permission to leave for Flanders," and the prince agreed to follow his friend's advice.

The door of the sanctuary opened, and the king and queen entered. Don Carlos bowed low. Elizabeth started at the sight of him, and the king gave him a somber look of suspicion.

The prince watched them pause before the tomb and move on out of sight.

"She is his! I have lost her!" he cried.

Rodrigo tried to console him, and they pledged their friendship and loyalty to each other.

Outside the monastery gates was a park where pages and ladies of the court had sought shelter from the sun. The page, Thibault, entered with Princess Eboli, lady-in-waiting to the queen.

While they waited for Elizabeth, Eboli and the others passed the time by singing the Moorish Song of the Veil.

Elizabeth came and seated herself among them. Rodrigo appeared and presented her with a letter that her mother had entrusted to him in Paris. At the same time he secretly pressed a note into her hand.

Eboli began asking him questions about the French court. During their conversation, Elizabeth read the note. It was from Don Carlos, asking her to place full trust in the bearer of the message.

She thanked Rodrigo and invited him to ask any favor of her.

"I will ask, but not for myself," he said. "I seek help for Don Carlos, who suffers from some unknown grief."

Eboli, listening, asked herself, "Could he possibly be in love with me?"

Rodrigo said to Elizabeth, "Grant him permission to see you."

"If the prince loves me, why does he hide it?" wondered Eboli.

Elizabeth sent Thibault to bring Don Carlos. Rodrigo led

Eboli away. Thibault came back with Don Carlos, and the page and the other attendants withdrew.

Outwardly calm at first, the prince told Elizabeth of his unhappiness at court. "I must leave," he said. "Ask the king to send me to Flanders."

Her heart was touched. "My son!" she said.

"Not that name!" he burst out, and he asked her to pity him in his wretchedness.

Elizabeth answered with dignity that she would carry his request to the king. "If he wishes Flanders to be in your command," she said, "you will surely be allowed to leave tomorrow."

He accused her of cold indifference.

"You should understand my silence," she said. "If we

were free to be together, the earth would seem like heaven."

Throwing aside all restraint, he cried out that he loved her. He tried to take her in his arms.

She pushed him away. "Go and kill your father!" she said fiercely. "Then, with his blood on your hands, lead your mother to the altar!"

The prince was shocked and sobered by the picture she painted. He turned and fled.

"God has saved us," she said faintly, kneeling to pray.

Thibault came from the monastery with word that the king was on his way.

Philip entered and was displeased to find that the queen had been left alone, in disobedience to his command. "Which lady should have been attending you?" he asked.

The Countess d'Aremberg came tremblingly forward, and Philip ordered her back to France.

Eboli, the other ladies-in-waiting, and Rodrigo had returned. They whispered to one another that by dismissing the countess, Philip was insulting the queen.

Elizabeth comforted the weeping countess, and all went away except Rodrigo and the king.

Philip asked, "Why have you never tried to speak with me? I know how to reward those who defend my interests, and you have faithfully served the crown."

Rodrigo answered that he was quite content and had no need of favors, except for others.

"What do you mean?" asked the king.

"I have come from Flanders, that was once so beautiful," said Rodrigo. "Now, under Spain's harsh rule, the land is like a tomb."

Philip defended the policy of Spain. Peace for the world, he said, could be bought only with blood.

"A horrible peace!" said Rodrigo, carried away by his feelings. "May history never say of you, 'He was a Nero!' Is this the peace you offer, where the priest is an executioner and the soldier is a bandit in armor? With the gift of freedom you could bring happiness to the world."

Philip answered cynically, "You will not speak so when you know men's hearts as I do. No more now. I have heard nothing. Do not fear. But beware the Grand Inquisitor!" Far from being angry, the king respected the young man's honesty. "I should like to have you near me at court," he said.

"Sir! No!" protested Rodrigo. "Let me remain as I am."

"You are too proud," said Philip. "You have dared to search out the trials of my kingdom. Now learn of the afflictions of the head that bears the crown. The queen— I am torn by suspicion— My son—"

Rodrigo said quickly, "His soul is proud and pure."

"Nothing can ever replace the blessing he has stolen from me!" said the king. He told Rodrigo, "I confide their destiny to you. Read what is in their hearts. I place my trust in you." He repeated in a tone of foreboding, "Beware the Grand Inquisitor. Beware!"

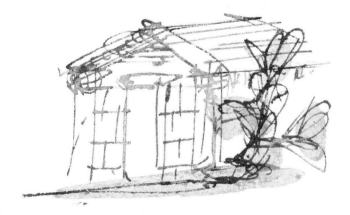

ACT III

Don Carlos waited in the queen's garden in Madrid. By moonlight he read again the note he had received: "At midnight in the garden, under the laurels near the fountain . . . ."

It was unsigned, but he was sure it came from Elizabeth, and he watched impatiently for her to appear.

A veiled figure came toward him. He greeted her ardently.

"Oh, may love bind your heart to mine forever!" she said, removing her veil.

"Oh, heaven!" he exclaimed.

It was not the queen. It was Eboli. She had written the note, wishing to warn him of conspiracies against him. "I can save you," she said. "I love you—I love you!"

"You have a noble heart, but I cannot accept the happiness you offer," he said. This meeting, he told her, was only a strange dream on a lovely night.

She realized the truth. "You thought you were speaking to another. You love the queen! You!"

Rodrigo had come into the garden, and he intervened to protect his friend. "You must not believe what he says. He is insane."

"Don Carlos' fate is in my hands," she said furiously, "and I'll have my revenge!"

"You shall die!" said Rodrigo, drawing a dagger. Don Carlos held him back.

Eboli warned the prince that he would not escape her

wrath. He said wildly to himself, "She knows all!" and Rodrigo threatened her with the punishment of God unless she kept silent.

She fled from the garden. Rodrigo told Don Carlos, "If you have any secret papers, entrust them to me."

"To you, confidant of the king?" returned Don Carlos.

"Are you suspicious of me?" asked Rodrigo.

Don Carlos was ashamed of his momentary doubt. "No," he said. "I place myself in your hands," and again Rodrigo promised his loyalty.

Crowds were gathering in the great square before the cathedral. Beyond was another square in which a pyre had been built for burning heretics at the stake. While monks dragged in the condemned prisoners, bells rang and the people shouted the praises of their king.

Ladies, gentlemen, and pages entered the square. Elizabeth and the page, Thibault, were among them. Rodrigo was there.

The cathedral doors were ceremoniously opened, revealing King Philip. He took his place beside the queen.

Suddenly Don Carlos was in the square, leading a group of men dressed in mourning.

Philip asked, "Who are they?"

"Envoys from Flanders and Brabant," answered his son.

The black-clad men spoke, begging mercy for the oppressed people of their land.

"You have offended God and rebelled against your king," said Philip, and he ordered his guards to remove the envoys.

Elizabeth, Thibault, Don Carlos, and Rodrigo spoke out

in defense of the men. People in the crowd asked the king to be merciful. But the monks declared that the men were traitors and deserved to die.

Don Carlos addressed his father, "If God wills that I shall some day wear your crown, let me prepare to be a worthy king. Let me rule Brabant and Flanders."

Philip imperiously refused his son's request.

The prince raised his sword in defiance and swore that he would be the savior of the Flemish people. Philip ordered him disarmed, but the guards drew back before Don Carlos.

Philip unsheathed his own sword.

Rodrigo intervened. The prince surrendered his weapon to his friend, who handed it to the king.

Philip was pleased with this action of his confidant and rewarded him with the title of duke.

The celebration continued. The royal couple proceeded to the places reserved for them, and flames rose from the great pyre.

ACT IV

King Philip sat alone in his study. The candles on the
table before him had burned low. Dawn had begun to
light the room.

Thinking of Elizabeth, he mused in bitter hopelessness,
"She never loved me. No, that heart is closed to me." Wear-
iness and sorrow were his lot, and rest would come to him
only when he lay in his tomb.

Count di Lerma entered and announced the Grand Inquisitor.

The Inquisitor, ninety years old and blind, came into the
study, supported by two friars. He asked, "Am I before
the king?"

"Yes, I sent for you. I am in doubt," said Philip. "Carlos
has taken up arms against me."

"How will you punish him?" asked the Grand Inquisitor.

"By exile or the axe," said Philip. "If I send my son to his
death, will you absolve me?"

The Inquisitor replied that the peace of the empire was
worth a traitor's life, and all scruples must be stilled to
uphold the faith.

"Very well," said the king.

"Have you nothing more to ask me?" said the Inquisitor.

"No," said Philip.

"Then I must speak to you," said the Grand Inquisitor,
and he denounced Rodrigo as a heretic, an enemy of the
church.

Philip spoke in defense of his friend, but the Inquisitor
demanded that Rodrigo be handed over to the Inquisition.

"No, never!" said the king.

The Inquisitor called the king a madman. "You would destroy the labor of years," he said, and he went away.

"So must the throne always bow to the altar," the king said to himself.

Elizabeth came into the study. Wounded and indignant, she reported that her jewel-case had been stolen. Then, at the terrible expression on the king's face, she paused. He went to the table and picked up the jewel-case. He handed it to her and ordered her to open it.

She shook her head.

"Then I will," he said. He broke open the case. Inside was a picture of Don Carlos.

Elizabeth fell in a faint.

"Help for the queen!" he called, and Rodrigo and Eboli rushed in.

Rodrigo said sternly to the king, "You are ruler of half the earth. Are you the only one you are not able to command?"

Philip said to himself, "I am accursed by this deadly suspicion. No—she has been true to me."

"I have ruined her!" Eboli was saying in deep remorse.

And Rodrigo was thinking, "The hour has come. Let me die for Spain. I shall bequeath her a happy future."

Elizabeth was regaining consciousness. The king hesitated, then left the study. Rodrigo followed him.

Eboli threw herself at the queen's feet and asked forgiveness.

Elizabeth was bewildered. "What have you done?" she asked.

Eboli confessed that it was she who had stolen the jewel-case, she who had accused the queen. "It was jealousy," she wept. "I loved Carlos, and he rejected me . . . . Have pity on me. Another fault—"

"Another?" said Elizabeth.

"The crime I accused you of—I myself have committed—with the king," said Eboli.

"You will leave the court," said Elizabeth. "You may choose either exile or the veil."

She went away.

Eboli was crushed with grief and shame. Because of her fatal gift of beauty, she had been proud and vain. Now she could only try to atone to heaven for her sins. The realization that she had sent Don Carlos to his death was unbearable to her. Perhaps, she thought, there might still be a way to save him.

Don Carlos had been imprisoned. Rodrigo came to the prison cell to bid his friend farewell. "This is my last hour. We shall never see each other again," he told the prince. "I have turned the threat upon myself. The king's rival is no longer you. It is I."

"Who will believe that?" asked Don Carlos.

"Your papers have been found in my possession," said Rodrigo. "They are proof of revolt and rebellion. Already there is a price on my head."

While he was speaking, two men came quietly down the stairs that led to the dungeon. One wore the garb of an official of the Inquisition. The other carried a handgun. They pointed out Don Carlos and Rodrigo to each other.

Don Carlos said to his friend, "I shall tell the king everything."

"No," said Rodrigo. "You must save yourself for the sake of Flanders. You were meant to rule. I was meant to die for you."

The man with the handgun took aim and fired. Rodrigo fell. "Listen—the queen waits for you tomorrow at St. Just," he said. "Do not forget me. Save Flanders— Farewell!"

He died, and Don Carlos, weeping, threw himself across the body of his friend.

Philip, with the Grand Inquisitor and a group of courtiers, came into the dungeon.

"My son," said the king, holding out his arms, "I give you back your sword."

Don Carlos said in revulsion, "Stand back. Your hand is stained with blood!"

Philip looked sorrowfully on the body of Rodrigo.

"I am your son no longer," said Don Carlos.

A warning bell began to ring. An angry crowd of people broke into the dungeon. They had come to free the prince. Eboli was with them, her face concealed by a mask.

The Grand Inquisitor revealed himself. "Kneel before the king, whom God protects!" he ordered.

Cowed and frightened before his wrath, the mob knelt, crying, "Lord, have mercy!" and the courtiers shouted, "Long live the king!"

ACT V

Elizabeth had come to St. Just. She was to meet Don Carlos in the cloister and send him away forever.

Kneeling in the moonlight before the tomb of Charles V, she remembered France and the happiness that had once been hers. Now she wished only for the peace that the grave could bring.

Don Carlos came into the cloister.

"A word only," she said. "Live and forget."

He answered that life without love was a living death.

"No," she said. "Think of Rodrigo. He did not give his life for a foolish idea."

Don Carlos told her of his plan to raise a monument in Flanders to the memory of Rodrigo. He bade her good-by, for the first time calling her his mother.

"Good-by, my son," she said.

But before they could part, the king was there, with the Grand Inquisitor and officers of the Inquisition.

Seeing Don Carlos and the queen alone together, Philip laid hands on his son. "I shall exact a double sacrifice!" he said.

"The Holy Inquisition will perform its duty," said the Grand Inquisitor, and the guards moved to seize the prince.

Don Carlos turned to defend himself. A grating opened beside the tomb. In the opening appeared the mysterious friar in royal mantle and crown.

He spoke: "The anguish of the earth follows us even in the cloister. Only in heaven will the heart find peace."

The Grand Inquisitor cried out, "It is the voice of Charles!" and the others exclaimed, "It is Charles V!"

"Oh, heaven!" cried Elizabeth, as the friar drew Don Carlos to safety within the cloister.

Otello

AFTER FINISHING *Aida in 1871, Giuseppe Verdi composed no more operas for the next fifteen years. Then a libretto by his friend Arrigo Boïto drew him out of retirement. Boïto's text was based on Shakespeare's* Othello. *Verdi's* Otello *was first performed at La Scala in Milan on February 5, 1887. The new work by the old master was acclaimed as one of the greatest of all his operas.*

ACT I

TOWARD THE END of the fifteenth century, when Cyprus was an outpost of Venice, the Venetians were at war with the Turks. Otello, the Moor, governor of Cyprus, had sailed against the Turkish fleet. Now Cypriots and Venetians waited along the quay near the governor's palace, watching for his return.

It was evening. A storm was raging, and lightning flashes revealed Otello's ship as it sailed into the harbor and cast anchor. Otello came up onto the quay. He called out the news that the enemy was defeated and buried in the sea, and to the cheers of the people, he went on into his palace.

Among the crowds were two Venetians—Iago, Otello's aide, and Roderigo, a young gentleman.

"What are you thinking?" asked Iago.

"Of drowning myself," answered Roderigo.

Iago said scornfully that anyone was a fool to take his life because of a woman. The beautiful Desdemona would

soon tire of the savage Moor she had married, "And," said
Iago, "I swear she shall be yours." He hated the Moor, he
told Roderigo, and with good reason. He pointed to Cassio,
a young captain standing near-by. "He holds the rank that
I have earned in a hundred battles," said Iago. "This is
Otello's will."

The two men moved away.

Some of the people had built a bonfire. Crowds gathered
about it, singing and drinking, as the storm passed. Iago,
Roderigo, and Cassio met at a table where wine was being
poured.

Iago persuaded Cassio to drink to the marriage of Otello
and Desdemona.

"She is the flower of this island," said Cassio, and he
praised Desdemona's loveliness.

"Listen to him," Iago said in a low voice to Roderigo.
"He will get in your path."

He pressed wine on Cassio, who had grown louder and
more abandoned. During this time Iago was urging Roderigo to pick a quarrel with the other man. It would cause
a riot, he said, thus interrupting Otello's reunion with
Desdemona.

Montano, former governor of Cyprus, came out of the
palace and spoke to Cassio, "The guard waits for you on
the ramparts."

Cassio started off, staggering from the wine he had
drunk. Montano looked at him, surprised and displeased.
Iago told the former governor confidentially, "Every night
he is like this."

Roderigo began to laugh.

"Who is laughing?" demanded Cassio.

"I am laughing at a drunkard," said Roderigo.

Cassio threw himself angrily upon Roderigo. Montano separated them.

Cassio turned on Montano and drew his sword, forcing the other man to defend himself.

Iago instructed Roderigo to go about the harbor and spread confusion. As Roderigo ran off, Iago spoke in an anxious voice, "Brothers! You must stop!"

A riot broke out among the people. Otello appeared and commanded them to put down their swords.

The fight ended. Otello asked Iago what had happened. Iago pretended not to know.

Cassio, sobered, began to apologize. Montano said, "I am wounded."

"Wounded!" exclaimed Otello. "By heaven . . . !"

Desdemona entered, and he went to her, angry that she had been roused from sleep. He said to Cassio, "You are no longer captain."

Cassio let his sword fall. Triumphantly Iago picked it up and handed it to an officer.

Otello sent the people back to their homes, and he and Desdemona were left alone on the quay. In her arms, he was calm again. She asked tenderly if he remembered the times when he had told her of his adventures and sufferings.

"You loved me for the dangers I had passed," he said, "and I loved you that you did pity them."

She prayed to heaven that their love would never change.

"A kiss," he said, kissing her. "A kiss . . . another kiss."

"The night is late," she said, and side by side they walked slowly toward the palace.

ACT II

In the palace Iago talked with Cassio, who stood on the garden terrace outside the doorway. It was through Desdemona, Iago was saying, that Cassio must seek to get back into Otello's good graces.

"How can I speak to her?" asked Cassio.

"It is her custom to walk under the trees with my wife," Iago told him. "Wait for her." Then, when Cassio had gone into the garden, Iago said reflectively, "Already I see your fate. Your demon drives you on, and I am your demon." He confessed to himself the creed by which he lived: "I believe in a cruel God, who has created me in his image." He believed himself fated to achieve his destiny through evil. As for life, it was nothing more than a mockery, death was oblivion, and heaven was an ancient lie!

Desdemona entered the garden with Iago's wife, Emilia. Cassio bowed to Desdemona and spoke to her.

Otello came upon Iago, who pretended to be disturbed at the sight of Desdemona and Cassio together. Craftily Iago played on the Moor's jealousy until Otello's suspicions were aroused.

Desdemona and Cassio had left the garden. Now she returned, surrounded by people of the island. They were offering her gifts and singing to her—a song of love and admiration. When the island people had gone, Desdemona and Emilia came into the palace.

As soon as Desdemona saw Otello she spoke to him of Cassio. "His grief is so real that it deserves forgiveness," she said. "Pardon him."

"Not now," he said.

His voice sounded strange to her. "What is wrong?" she asked.

He answered that his head ached. She tried to bind his forehead with her handkerchief. He seized the handkerchief and threw it aside.

Desdemona was hurt and bewildered, not knowing how she had offended him. Emilia picked up the handkerchief. In a whisper Iago asked her to give it to him. She whispered back, asking what possible use it could be to him, and he wrenched the handkerchief out of her hand.

Desdemona was asking Otello's pardon. Impatiently he ordered her to leave him. She went, with Emilia following.

Otello could no longer control himself. He lashed out at Iago, saying that suspicion was worse than the most dreadful injury and demanding proof that Desdemona was unfaithful.

Iago answered that he had heard Cassio talk in his sleep, speaking Desdemona's name and saying, "Let our love be secret." He asked, "Have you not seen in your wife's hand a fine-textured handkerchief embroidered with flowers?"

"It was my gift to her," said Otello.

"Yesterday I am certain I saw that handkerchief in the hand of Cassio," said Iago.

With a terrible curse, Otello knelt and swore that he would be avenged. Iago, kneeling beside him, joined in the oath.

ACT III

In the great hall of the palace Otello and Iago were speaking earnestly together. A herald entered. A Venetian galley was in the harbor bringing ambassadors to Cyprus, he reported.

When the herald had gone, Otello and Iago resumed their conversation. "I will bring Cassio here," said Iago. "Stay hidden and mark his words and manner."

He saw Desdemona approaching, and as he left, he reminded Otello of the handkerchief.

Desdemona entered and brought up the subject of Cassio.

"My headache comes upon me again," said Otello, and he asked her to bind his forehead. She offered him a handkerchief. "No, I would have the one I gave you," he said.

"I do not have it about me," she said.

The handkerchief was enchanted, he told her. To lose it or give it away was terrible misfortune.

"You frighten me," she said.

"What? Have you lost it?" he asked.

"No," she answered.

"Go fetch it," he said.

"Presently," she said.

She tried to tell him that Cassio was his dear friend and worthy of pardon.

"The handkerchief . . . the handkerchief!" Otello broke in.

She recognized the fury in his voice, and she begged to know what she had done.

He accused her of being unfaithful. Then, with ironic politeness, he took her hand, led her to the doorway, and suddenly pushed her outside.

Alone, he gave way to jealous rage.

Iago returned. "Cassio is there," he said.

Otello concealed himself behind a pillar. Iago brought Cassio into the hall.

"I had hoped Desdemona would be here," said Cassio.

"He speaks her name!" said Otello.

"I would speak with her," went on Cassio, "to know if my pardon has been granted."

"Wait for her," said Iago. "Meanwhile, tell me something of the one you adore."

"Of whom?" asked Cassio.

Iago mentioned a girl with whom Cassio's name had been linked. "Of Bianca," he said in an undertone.

Cassio began to laugh.

Otello, who had not heard Bianca's name, was sure that the conversation was about Desdemona and that Cassio was laughing in triumph.

Cassio told a tale of a beautiful handkerchief that had been mysteriously left in his lodgings. Iago led him away from the pillar so that their words were lost to Otello.

"Do you have it with you?" asked Iago.

Cassio held up the handkerchief. Iago examined it and managed to pass it behind his back so that it could be seen by Otello.

While Cassio admired the handkerchief, Iago was thinking, "This is a web in which your heart is caught and dies." And to himself, Otello was crying out, "Treachery! Treason!"

A fanfare of trumpets sounded, then a cannon shot, heralding the arrival of the Venetian galley.

Iago sent Cassio away. Otello came out of hiding.

"Did you hear how he laughed?" said Iago. "And the handkerchief—?"

"She is condemned!" said Otello.

"And I'll provide for Cassio," promised Iago.

"From this time on, you are my captain," Otello said.

"I give you my thanks," said Iago. The ambassadors were outside. "Receive them," he told Otello, "but to avoid suspicion, let Desdemona be present."

He left, and Otello prepared to greet the visitors.

Lodovico, chief ambassador, entered with Roderigo, soldiers, and ladies and gentlemen of the court. Iago escorted Desdemona and Emilia into the hall.

Lodovico delivered the message sent to Otello by the doge of Venice; then he, Desdemona, and Iago formed a group and stood talking. The ambassador asked why Cassio was not present.

"Otello is annoyed with him," replied Iago.

"He will be back in favor," predicted Desdemona.

Otello, reading the doge's letter, spoke so that only she could hear, "Are you sure?"

"Perhaps he will be back in favor," said Iago.

"I hope so," said Desdemona innocently. "You know the affection I feel for Cassio."

"You devil, be silent!" shouted Otello, leaping to his feet and striking at her.

Lodovico held him back. Desdemona began to weep.

Otello said to a herald, "Bring Cassio to me."

The herald brought Cassio into the hall. Otello raised his voice so that all could hear. "The doge has recalled me to Venice. My successor in Cyprus is Cassio."

Iago exclaimed in an undertone, "Hell and death!"

"The populace and the army and navy and the fortress I leave in the hands of the new governor," continued Otello. He said to Lodovico and Desdemona, "We shall sail tomorrow."

Desdemona was still in tears. "Kneel—and weep!" he cried, brutally forcing her to her knees.

She lamented his lost love. Emilia, Cassio, Roderigo, and Lodovico looked on in pity. Under cover of the confusion, Iago tried to spur Otello to action. "Quick! Direct yourself to the matter at hand," he said. "I'll see to Cassio." He turned to Roderigo and reminded him, "Tomorrow your love will be on the high seas."

"Ah, sadness!" exclaimed Roderigo.

"You can still hope," said Iago. Cassio was the new governor, it was true, but if some misfortune should befall him before the ship sailed, then Otello and Desdemona would stay.

Roderigo was frightened and apprehensive, yet he agreed to kill Cassio at the time and place appointed by Iago.

Otello's anger had burst out again, and he drove the people from the hall, hurling a last curse after Desdemona. A convulsion seized him, and he fell to the floor.

From outside came the voices of Cypriots shouting, "Long live Otello! Glory to the lion of Venice!"

Iago looked down at the inert figure and said in a tone of contemptuous triumph, "Here is the lion!"

ACT IV

That night Desdemona waited in her bedchamber for Otello. She said to Emilia, "Lay out my bridal garments, and if I should die before you, let me be buried in one of those veils."

Emilia begged her to put such thoughts from her mind.

Sitting before the mirror, Desdemona recalled a maid-servant in her mother's home—poor Barbara, who had been deserted by her lover. "She sang a song—the willow song," said Desdemona. "Tonight it will not leave my mind."

She began to sing the melancholy song. She took a ring from her finger and gave it to Emilia, saying, "Put it away." Once she thought she heard a wailing outside and a knocking at the door, but Emilia said reassuringly that it was only the wind.

Desdemona finished singing poor Barbara's song. She bade Emilia farewell, her voice rising in a tragic cry.

Emilia left her. Desdemona knelt at the prie-dieu, above
which hung a picture of the Blessed Virgin, and after she
had prayed, she went to bed.

Otello entered by way of a secret door. He laid his sword
on the table and put out the candle. The room was lighted
only by the lamp that burned before the picture of the
Virgin.

Standing by the bed, he looked down at Desdemona. He
bent and kissed her three times. At the last kiss, she wakened.

"Who is there? Otello?" she asked.

"Yes," he said. He asked if she had prayed that her sins
might be forgiven. "I would not kill your soul," he said.

"Do you talk of killing?" she asked.

"Yes," he said.

She pleaded for her life.

"You love Cassio," he said. "That handkerchief I gave to
you, you gave to him."

"It is not true," she cried.

"In his own hands I saw it," he said.

She protested her innocence and asked that Cassio be
brought to vindicate her. He answered that Cassio was
dead.

"Let me live tonight," she implored him. "An hour . . .
an instant . . . long enough for a prayer."

It was too late, said Otello. Silencing her last plea, he
strangled her.

There was a knocking at the door. "Open!" called Emilia.

"Who is there?" asked Otello.

"My lord, let me speak to you," said Emilia.

He opened the door, admitting her. A great crime had

been committed, she told him. Cassio had killed Roderigo.

"And Cassio?" he asked.

"Cassio lives," she said.

Desdemona cried out faintly. Emilia went to the bed.

"I die innocent," said Desdemona.

Emilia said in horror, "Who has done this?"

"No one . . . only myself . . . farewell," said Desdemona, as she died.

"Liar!" exclaimed Otello. "It was I who killed her. She loved Cassio. Iago told me."

"Iago! And you believed him?" Emilia ran to the door, calling wildly for help.

Lodovico, Cassio, and Iago entered. Montano followed with guards. Emilia demanded that her husband clear Desdemona's name.

"I believed her guilty," replied Iago.

Otello spoke again of the handkerchief. "She gave it to Cassio," he said.

Emilia started to speak, and Iago warned her to be quiet.

"No!" she said. She told the others, "This man forced the handkerchief from me."

"And I found it in my room," said Cassio.

Montano said, looking at Iago, "The dying Roderigo revealed this man's vile scheming."

Iago fled. The guards followed in pursuit.

Otello took up his sword and let it fall. He looked on Desdemona's face. In a broken voice he spoke her name. Then he drew a dagger and stabbed himself.

He bent over the figure on the bed. "I kissed you before I killed you," he said. "Now, dying—a kiss . . . another kiss . . . one more kiss," and with the last kiss, he died.

Falstaff

THROUGHOUT *most of his long operatic career, Giuseppe Verdi had written only tragedies. His last opera, Falstaff, finished when he was almost eighty, was a miracle of comedy. His friend Boïto furnished the libretto, basing his story on two of Shakespeare's plays,* The Merry Wives of Windsor *and* King Henry IV.

Falstaff was first performed at La Scala in Milan on February 9, 1893, and was hailed as one of the three or four great masterpieces of comic opera.

ACT I

THE PLACE was the town of Windsor near London. The time was during the reign of Henry IV. Sir John Falstaff, fat, good-natured, and unprincipled, sat in the Garter Inn, a favorite meeting-place for him and his roistering friends. He had just written and sealed two letters and settled back to drink at his ease, when Dr. Caius came storming in.

"You have beaten my servants!" shouted the physician. "You have ridden my bay mare and broken into my house!"

Falstaff calmly admitted his guilt.

Nearby was Bardolph, Falstaff's red-nosed drinking companion. Dr. Caius turned on him. "Last night you made me drink," he said, "and when I was drunk, you picked my pockets."

"Not I," said Bardolph.

"Who then?" asked the doctor.

Falstaff called to Pistol, another of his companions, and asked him, "Did you pick the gentleman's pockets?"

"Of course he did," said Dr. Caius.

"You lie!" said Pistol, and he brandished a broom at the doctor.

The two exchanged furious insults. Falstaff tried to restore order. "Now who was it," he asked, "who picked this
gentleman's pockets?"

"He drinks too much," said Bardolph, indicating the doctor, "then he comes up with some fable he dreamed while
he was sleeping under the table."

"There, you've had the truth," said Falstaff. "Now go in
peace."

And Dr. Caius went, vowing that if he ever drank again,
it would be with decent, sober people.

Falstaff reproved his two companions for their clumsi-
ness in the art of stealing. Then, looking at the innkeeper's
bill, he complained to his friends, "You are my destruction.
Your drinking costs me too much. You make me lose weight,
and if Falstaff grows thin, no one will love him any more."
They must sharpen their wits, he said, and find a way to in-
crease their fortune. "Do you know a townsman named
Ford?" he asked.

Bardolph and Pistol both knew him.

"He is rich," said Falstaff. "His wife is beautiful."

"And she keeps the money-box," said Pistol.

"Alice is her name," said Falstaff. He told how he had
seen her one day, how she had gazed at him in admiration.
There was another townswoman named Meg. She, too, admired him, and she, too, held the keys to the family coffers.

He took up the two letters he had written and handed
one to Bardolph. "Take this to Meg," he said.

The other letter was to Alice. He asked Pistol to take it
to her.

With dignity, as befitting honorable men, Bardolph and
Pistol refused to deliver the letters.

A page had just come in. Falstaff gave the letters to him. "Take these at once," he said, and to Bardolph and Pistol he held forth scathingly on the subject of honor. What was honor? Could it fill an empty stomach? Could it mend a broken leg? Honor was only a fine word. "I'll have none of it!" he said in a thunderous voice. "As for you two scoundrels, I've endured you too long. Now I'm finished with you." And he seized the broom and drove them out of the inn.

Mistress Page, known as Meg, and her friend, Dame Quickly, had come to the home of Mistress Ford. Alice Ford and her daughter, Anne, were just leaving the house. The four met in the garden.

"I have a letter," said Meg.

"I, too," said Alice.

The two women displayed their letters, both declarations of love, both from Sir John Falstaff.

"Monster!" said Dame Quickly, and the women began to plan their revenge on the vain and ridiculous knight.

They went away together. Alice's husband, with Bardolph and Pistol, came upon the scene. Dr. Caius and Fenton, a young gentleman, followed the other men into the garden.

Dr. Caius was denouncing Falstaff. Bardolph and Pistol were telling Ford that Falstaff was hatching a plot against him. Fenton said that nothing would please him more than to bring the fat knight to his senses.

Ford asked them to speak one at a time so that he could understand.

Pistol informed him that Falstaff had written a letter to Alice.

"I'll look after my wife and the gentleman," Ford promised him. "I'll protect my home."

The four women returned to the garden. Anne and Fenton exchanged affectionate glances.

Alice, looking at her husband, said, "If he only knew—"

"Is Ford jealous?" asked Meg.

"Yes!" answered Alice.

"Quiet," said Dame Quickly, and the three women went away, leaving Anne in the garden. Ford, Bardolph, Pistol, and the doctor walked on. Fenton stayed behind.

"Come here," he whispered to Anne.

"What do you want?" she asked.

"Two kisses," he said.

Hastily they kissed, then he started off, as the women returned.

Alice was considering sending an answer to Falstaff's letter. Anne suggested that a visit might be better, and Dame Quickly was elected to go to Falstaff with the promise of a meeting with Alice.

Fenton had reappeared in another part of the garden. Dame Quickly thought someone had come to spy on them, and she, Meg, and Alice ran away. Anne stayed for a word with Fenton.

But they had only a few moments together before her father, Dr. Caius, Bardolph, and Pistol came back. Anne left, and Fenton joined the other men.

Ford was asking where Falstaff lived.

"At the Garter Inn," said Pistol.

"Go announce me to him under a false name," said Ford.

The women returned. In one side of the garden they talked of the revenge they would have on Falstaff. Meanwhile, Dr. Caius, Ford, Pistol, and Bardolph were trying to decide on the best way to deal with the amorous knight. Fenton stood apart, looking across at Anne and telling himself, "She must soon belong to me."

The men left together. The women took leave of one another. Alice quoted a tender line from Falstaff's letter, and they all burst out laughing.

ACT II

In the Garter Inn Falstaff sat drinking sack. Bardolph and Pistol had returned to him, pretending to be penitent and humble. Bardolph reported that a woman was outside, waiting to see him.

"Let her in," said Falstaff.

Bardolph brought in Dame Quickly.

Falstaff sent Bardolph and Pistol away, and Dame Quickly gave him a message from Alice: "She thanks you for your letter, and you may go freely to her home between two and three."

"Tell her I shall be impatiently awaiting the hour," said Falstaff.

Dame Quickly also brought an affectionate message from Meg. Falstaff asked if each woman had kept her letter a secret from the other.

"Do not fear," said Dame Quickly, and Falstaff gave her a coin and dismissed her.

"Alice is mine!" he said, and he congratulated himself on the charm that made him irresistible.

Bardolph announced a Mr. Brook, who was Ford in disguise.

Ford introduced himself as a wealthy man.

"Dear Mr. Brook," said Falstaff. "We must become better acquainted."

Ford put down a bag of money. "Here in Windsor there is a beautiful lady named Alice, wife of a certain Ford," he said. He loved her madly, but she would have none of him.

"Why do you tell me this?" asked Falstaff.

Ford explained. Falstaff was a gentleman, a man of the world. "There is a bag of money. Spend it—be rich and happy. In exchange, win Alice for me."

Falstaff accepted the money. In half an hour he would be seeing Ford's wife, he said. She had just sent word that her blockhead of a husband was out between two and three.

He asked Ford to wait for him. Clutching the moneybag, he waddled off to make himself presentable for his visit with Alice.

Ford's assurance had been shaken. Could it be that his wife was deceiving him? In jealous anger he told himself that he would keep watch on this villain and have his revenge.

Falstaff came back wearing a new doublet and a hat and carrying a cane. He invited Ford to walk part of the way with him, and they went out together.

At the Fords' house Dame Quickly was telling Alice, Meg, and Anne what had happened at the inn. "He fell into the trap," she said. "You'll see him here between two and three."

"Everything is ready," said Alice, and she called two servants to bring the laundry basket. She, Meg, and Dame Quickly were delighted at the sport they would soon be making of the fat knight, but Anne looked sad. She loved young Fenton, she said, but her father had decided that she was to marry Dr. Caius.

The others were shocked at the idea, and Alice told her not to be afraid.

Two servants brought in a huge basket of soiled laundry. Alice instructed them, "When I call you, empty it into the gutter."

The women set the scene. They placed a screen between the fireplace and the laundry basket.

Dame Quickly saw Falstaff coming up to the house. She, Anne, and Meg left the room. Alice took up her lute and was plucking the strings when Falstaff entered.

"My beautiful Alice!" he said, and he confessed to a guilty thought. He wished that Ford might pass on to a better life. "Then," he said, "you would be my lady, and I would be your lord."

"I am afraid you are deceiving me," she said. "I am afraid you are in love with Meg."

"I can't stand her face," he said.

Dame Quickly entered. "My lady, Mistress Meg is here," she said breathlessly, and rushed out again.

Falstaff hid behind the screen.

Meg appeared. With a show of agitation she told Alice that Ford was on his way home. "He is furious," she said. "He says a man is hiding here."

Dame Quickly returned. "Mistress Alice!" she cried, "Master Ford is coming. Save yourself. He is raving and threatening—"

Her manner worried Alice. "Is this true," she asked, so that Falstaff could not hear, "or is it part of the joke?"

"It's true!" said Dame Quickly. "He is coming into the garden. There's a crowd with him."

Falstaff started from behind the screen, thought better of it, and hid himself again.

Ford rushed into the room, leading Fenton, Dr. Caius, Bardolph, and Pistol. "Shut the doors! Block the stairway! Drive him out!" he shouted. Fenton, Bardolph, and Pistol went to search the adjoining rooms.

Alice confronted her husband. "Are you out of your mind?" she demanded.

"What is in that basket?" he asked.

"The wash," she said.

He handed Dr. Caius a bunch of keys and sent him to search the wardrobes and cupboards. He looked into the basket, scattering the linen about, then he dashed out into the next room.

Alice said to Meg and Dame Quickly that they must find a way to get Falstaff out of the house. She went to call the servants.

Falstaff came out from behind the screen.

"Sir John! You here?" cried Meg, pretending great amazement.

"I love you. I love you only. Save me!" he gasped, and he climbed into the basket. Meg and Dame Quickly covered him with the laundry.

Anne and Fenton entered softly and hid behind the screen for a few stolen moments together.

Ford and his search party returned, opening chests, looking into the fireplace, and unlocking the wardrobe. During a lull they heard the unmistakable sound of a kiss. The sound came from behind the screen.

"There he is!" Ford said.

"There he is!" said Dr. Caius.

Bardolph and Pistol came in with some of the neighbors who had joined the hunt. Ford pointed to the screen. "I've found him," he said in a whisper. "Falstaff is there with my wife."

Half-suffocating, Falstaff put his face out of the basket. Dame Quickly thrust him back under the clothes.

Behind the screen Fenton and Anne were exchanging confidences, oblivious of all that was happening about them.

Ford drew up a plan of attack and ranged his men in strategic positions.

"I am cooked . . . I want only a breath of air!" moaned Falstaff, trying to lift his head, and Dame Quickly pushed him down again.

The men were listening to the voices that came from behind the screen—plainly the conversation of a woman and her sweetheart.

"Filthy basket!" sputtered Falstaff. Alice had come quietly in and was standing near him. "Silence!" she said.

Ford gave the signal. He and his men overturned the screen, exposing Fenton and Anne. The lovers drew apart in confusion.

"Again you disobey me!" Ford raged at his daughter. And to Fenton, "I have told you she shall never be yours!"

Anne and Fenton fled in different directions. Ford and his search party hurried off to another part of the house.

Alice rang a bell. Anne came in with four servants and a page.

"Empty the basket through the window and into the ditch," directed Alice. "There—near those washerwomen." While the four servants struggled with the basket, Alice sent the page to bring her husband.

The servants lifted the basket and tipped Falstaff and the laundry into the ditch outside the window. There was a great shout. The washerwomen burst into cackles of laughter.

Ford and the other men had returned. Alice, thinking it was time to reveal that she had only been making sport of the ridiculous knight, led her husband to the window so that he might witness Falstaff's humiliation.

ACT III

Falstaff sat on a bench in front of the Garter Inn. "Evil world!" he muttered. "To have lived as long as I, then to be carried in a clothesbasket and be tossed into a ditch!" The realization came to him that he was too fat, that his hair was gray and he was growing old.

The innkeeper brought a large glass of steaming wine. Falstaff drank. Little by little he grew more cheerful.

Dame Quickly appeared. "The beautiful Alice—" she began.

"To the devil with your beautiful Alice!" he interrupted.
Behind a house near the inn Alice, Ford, Meg, Anne,
Fenton, and Dr. Caius were hiding. From time to time they
peered out to spy on Falstaff.

Dame Quickly said, "She is innocent. She loves you." She
gave him a letter from Alice.

Ford and his wife, watching, whispered, "He's reading."

Falstaff read the letter: " 'I shall await you in the Royal
Oak Park at midnight. Come in the disguise of the Black
Huntsman and wait at Herne's Oak.' "

Dame Quickly explained that Alice had chosen to meet
him in a mysterious, romantic setting. She began to tell him
the legend of the Black Huntsman. His good humor restored, Falstaff took her arm and they went into the inn.

Alice and the others came out from behind the house.
She continued the story of the Black Huntsman. At midnight, she said, the huntsman, who had been hanged in the
park, returned and wandered with the other spirits. It was
all nonsense, she added—only a tale used to frighten children.

Ford looked forward with relish to taking part in the
further humiliation of Falstaff.

"Take care," said his wife. "You, too, should be punished," and Ford asked forgiveness for his jealousy.

They planned the masquerade which was to take place
that night in the park. Anne would dress as the fairy queen,
all in white. Meg would be a wood nymph and Dame
Quickly a witch. There would be children masquerading as
imps, elves, and sprites. They would set upon Falstaff, said
Alice, and torment him until he begged for mercy.

Evening was coming on. The group separated and started

away. Dame Quickly came out of the inn and stopped to eavesdrop on Ford and Dr. Caius, who were holding a secret conference.

"Do not fear," said Ford. "You shall marry my daughter. Do you remember what she will wear?"

"A garland of roses and a white veil and dress," answered the doctor. He himself would dress as a monk, and the monk's cowl would conceal his face. During the masquerade he would lead Anne forward, and her father would pronounce them husband and wife.

Arm in arm, Ford and Dr. Caius walked away, and Dame Quickly looked knowingly after them.

Fenton was first at the meeting-place that night. He heard Anne's voice and went to meet her. She was dressed as the fairy queen. Meg and Dame Quickly arrived in their disguises.

Alice made Fenton put on the cape and mask she had brought.

"You look like a monk," said Anne.

"Ford's plan shall be turned against him," said Alice.

Fenton asked her to explain, but she refused, telling him only to obey in silence.

They all ran away as Falstaff approached. He wore a black cape and on his head were two staghorns. He paused under the oak. Alice came out of the woods.

"You are my lady!" he greeted her.

They were not alone here, she cautioned him. Meg was following her.

Meg entered, calling for help. "Here comes the witch!"

"Run!" cried Alice, and she ran off into the woods.

Falstaff flattened himself against the oak. Anne appeared with a group of girls dressed as fairies. The sight filled Falstaff with terror. He threw himself face down upon the ground.

Bardolph and Pistol entered in costume. Alice, Meg, and Dame Quickly followed. Dr. Caius was there in his cape, along with Ford, who was not in costume. Other townspeople had come to join the masquerade.

They all gathered about the prone figure. "A man!" they exclaimed in threatening tones, and Falstaff begged them to have mercy.

Dr. Caius had been searching for Anne. She eluded him and disappeared with Fenton.

Bardolph was pretending to be a sorcerer calling down wicked enchantments. Small boys dressed as imps were pinching Falstaff, sticking him with nettles, and rolling him over and over. Falstaff howled with pain and fright and cried out that he repented his sins.

Bardolph accidentally revealed his face. Falstaff recognized him and denounced his traitorous friend.

Dame Quickly spoke softly to Bardolph and led him away.

Ford bowed to Falstaff in an ironic gesture of respect. Alice and Meg unmasked. Falstaff was staring at Ford. "Dear Master Brook," he said.

"This is Ford, my husband," said Alice.

Dame Quickly had returned. Did Falstaff really fancy, she asked, that two women could have fallen in love with such a fat, evil creature as himself?

Now it was clear to Falstaff that he had been made a laughingstock. Trying to regain his self-possession, he reminded the others that although everyone jeered at him now, it was he who gave the situation its humor.

Ford was in a forgiving mood. "Enough of this," he said, and he told them all that the masquerade would be crowned by a wedding.

Dr. Caius had found Anne, as he thought, a veiled figure in white. Alice brought forward a second couple, veiled and masked, and Ford was pleased at the prospect of a double wedding.

"Heaven joins you in marriage," he said. "Now cast away your masks and veils."

The first couple unmasked. Dr. Caius found that his supposed bride was Bardolph, whom Dame Quickly had disguised. The second couple revealed themselves as Fenton and Anne.

"Confusion!" cried Dr. Caius.

"Treachery!" exclaimed Ford, and Falstaff bowed to him, asking sardonically, "Tell me now, who is the fool?"

Anne made a supplicating gesture to her father. "Forgive me," she said, and Ford was persuaded to bless her and Fenton.

"A cheer to end the play," said Falstaff.

"Then all to dine with Sir John Falstaff," said Ford, and the masquerade ended with a chorus in praise of laughter.

The Bartered Bride

BEDRICH SMETANA *was the first Bohemian composer to become world famous. The Bartered Bride, composed to a libretto by Karel Sabina, is his best known opera. It was first performed in Prague on May 30, 1866. For the following twenty-five years the opera was hardly known outside Bohemia. Then a performance in Vienna in 1892 quickly led to its world-wide popularity.*

ACT I

LONG AGO in Bohemia it was the custom for parents to arrange the marriages of their sons and daughters. Marie, a village girl, had been promised to the son of a wealthy peasant. At the village fair she tearfully broke the news to her sweetheart, Hans. Tobias Micha was bringing his son here today to marry her, she said.

Marie's parents favored Wenzel Micha as a son-in-law. They had never approved of Hans. He was a stranger in the village. They knew nothing of his past or parentage.

"And there does seem to be a mystery about you," admitted Marie.

There was no mystery, he said. He had lived happily until his mother died and his father married again. His stepmother had made life so unpleasant for him that he left home and made his own way. "But with a love as true as ours," he said, "we shall soon forget every misfortune."

Marie's parents and Kezal, the marriage broker, came into the square. Hans and Marie quickly said good-by and left in opposite directions.

"You gave your word and everything is as good as arranged," Kezal was saying, with an important air, "and if your daughter is unruly, she must learn a proper sense of duty."

Kruschina, Marie's father, was satisfied with the arrangement. Kathinka, her mother, had a lingering doubt, and she asked just what sort of husband this young man would make.

"What a question!" said the marriage broker. "I guarantee him." Furthermore, the boy's father was Tobias Micha, and Micha's farm was worth forty thousand crowns.

Kruschina had known Tobias Micha since they were boys together. He asked his wife, "Don't you remember him?"

"Of course," said Kathinka. "Didn't he have a son named Hans?"

The marriage broker spoke scornfully of Hans—a good-for-nothing vagabond who had turned against his family and disappeared. "No," he said, "the only son now is Wenzel." The broker praised his client—the young man was healthy and strong, he had wealth, and although he was not particularly subtle or shrewd, he was sure to make a dependable husband.

Marie came back into the square. Her parents and the broker told her about the fine young man who had been chosen for her, and Kezal offered a contract for her to sign.

"But there is someone else," said Marie.

Her word to someone else meant nothing, said Kezal. The two fathers had already signed the marriage contract.

"That doesn't concern me," said Marie, and she put an end to the discussion by running away.

Kezal was shocked at her willfulness. Kruschina wondered if they should not bring Marie and Wenzel together, so that the girl could see what an excellent husband had been chosen for her.

The broker agreed. However, the young man was shy. It

might be better if the two could meet more casually, as if by accident. "In the meantime," he said, "I'll find this man she mentions and deal with him."

He and Marie's parents left the square, as musicians struck up a polka and villagers danced.

ACT II

Hans had gone to the inn, where he sat drinking with a group of young men. Across the room from them was Kezal. The young villagers praised the ale for its gifts of courage and vigor. But only love, said Hans, would bring true happiness. And to that, said Kezal, should be added money.

Some of the villagers began to dance, and after the dancing everyone left the inn.

Wenzel, son of Tobias Micha, came hesitantly into the room. He was painfully shy, he stuttered, and his mother was pushing him into a marriage for which he was not quite ready.

Marie entered and spoke to him, "You must be the bridegroom of Marie Kruschina."

"Yes—but how—how did you know?" he stammered.

"Everyone knows, and everyone pities you," she said. Marie would lead him a life of torment, she told him. Besides, she could not be true because she loved someone else.

Wenzel was alarmed. "Mamma says I must marry," he said.

"Of course," she agreed, but there were many girls. There was even one who secretly loved him.

"Is she pretty?" asked Wenzel.

"As pretty as Marie," she answered.

"Is she young?" he asked.

"As young as Marie," she said. "Will you let her die, will you let her love you in vain?"

"No—no!" he said.

Then he must promise to give up Marie, she told him, and he raised his hand and solemnly swore that Marie was no longer betrothed to him.

They left together. Kezal and Hans came into the room. The marriage broker had found an ideal wife for the young man, and he described her as pretty, virtuous, and wealthy. "She can be yours," he said. "Only promise me that you will give up Marie."

Hans refused.

The broker persisted. Hans' promise would be worth three hundred gulden.

Hans said indignantly, "You could not buy Marie from me for a million!"

"I have one wife, and she is enough," said Kezal. "In this matter I am acting for Tobias Micha."

"Ah, that's different," said Hans, and he accepted the broker's offer. The only condition was that Marie marry the son of Tobias Micha and none other.

"That is understood," said the broker, and he hurried off to have the contract drawn up.

He came back bringing Kathinka, Kruschina, and a crowd of villagers.

"We will witness the contract," said the villagers, "but first let us hear the terms of it."

Kezal read the contract. Its terms called for Hans to give up his promised bride, provided that no one else claimed her except the son of Tobias Micha. In return, Hans was to receive three hundred gulden.

The villagers were outraged that a man would barter his bride for gold. "Shame! Dishonor!" they cried, as Hans cheerfully signed the contract.

ACT III

Wenzel sat alone and miserable in the square. The day's happenings had left him confused.

A company of strolling players entered. Among them were Springer, the manager, Muff, who played East Indian roles, and Esmeralda, a tightrope walker. Villagers flocked after them, and the manager announced the evening's performance.

Wenzel looked and listened in fascination. Esmeralda began to talk to him.

Muff drew the manager aside to inform him of a crisis. A member of the troupe, the man who impersonated the dancing bear, had drunk so much that he was not able to walk.

They noticed Esmeralda in conversation with a young man who looked as if the bearskin would fit him perfectly. Springer spoke to Wenzel and asked him to join the troupe.

Wenzel was overwhelmed.

"Please come, my darling," said Esmeralda. "I can teach you all you need to know."

The rest of the company had gone to advertise the coming performance. Esmeralda and the manager followed them. Wenzel was alone again and more confused than ever.

His mother, Agnes, entered, with Micha and the marriage broker.

"Wenzel will sign our contract," said Kezal, "and everything will be ready."

"Why must I sign it?" asked Wenzel.

"To say that you will marry Marie," explained his father.

Wenzel protested, "I don't want to marry her."

The others were astounded.

Someone had warned him against Marie, he said, and when they tried to question him, he ran away.

Marie and her parents came into the square. They had just told her of the contract Hans had signed—a contract renouncing her.

"It isn't true! I can't believe it!" she said.

Kezal displayed the signed document. "Three hundred gulden was his price," he said.

Marie was forced to believe that Hans had been false to her. But when Kezal asked her to sign a contract binding her to Wenzel, she cried out that she would never marry him.

"It's the only way," insisted the others.

Wenzel had not gone far, and Kezal brought him back. "Why do you keep calling me?" he asked. Then he saw Marie, and his sulky expression turned to one of delight. "There is the one who warned me!" he said.

"But she is Marie, your future wife," the others told him.

Without trying to puzzle out the riddle, Wenzel at once declared that she was the girl he was ready to marry.

Kezal said impatiently, "Then let the bond be signed."

Marie asked for time to think. Left alone, she meditated on her happiness with Hans and her grief without him.

Hans found her there. She turned away from him. "How could you be so low as to sign the bond?" she said.

"Be patient," he said calmly. "I can explain."

She ordered him to leave her, and now her decision was made. "Everything is over between us," she said. "I'm going to marry Wenzel!"

He began to laugh. Infuriated, Marie refused to wait for his explanation. As she started away, she collided with Kezal.

The marriage broker saw Hans and said to him, "Waiting for your money, are you? Just have patience."

"This is shameful!" cried Marie.

"Surely you've decided to marry Tobias Micha's son," said Kezal.

Hans spoke for her, "Certainly she has. No one else can have her," and Marie wept.

Kathinka and Kruschina appeared, with Agnes and Micha and a crowd of villagers. They asked Marie what she had decided.

She answered that she agreed to the terms of the con-

tract. The villagers began to plan the wedding feast.
Hans came forward. "Yes, prepare the feast," he said.

At the sight of him, Agnes and Micha cried out. Hans
said to Micha, "Well, Father, I've come home at last."

Kezal was nonplussed. "Can it be true," he asked, "that
this is the older son of Tobias Micha?"

"Yes, I am Micha's older son," said Hans. After years of
wandering, he said, he had decided to come back and make
a home for himself in his native village. He pointed out
that now, according to the terms of the contract, Marie—
and the three hundred gulden, as well—belonged to him.

At last Marie understood, and she threw herself into his
arms.

Kezal was dismayed to find that he had been outwitted,
and Agnes and Micha upbraided him.

While the villagers laughed at the turn of events, there
was a loud commotion just off the square. Boys came running in, shouting that the bear was loose.

A figure dressed in a bearskin came clumsily into the
square. "Don't be afraid," he said. "I am Wenzel."

"You idiot, what have you done!" said his mother.
"Come away from here and take off that masquerade."

Marie's father said to Micha, "Now then, my friend, you
surely realize that Wenzel would not make a proper husband for my daughter. He is still somewhat lacking in
reason. Remember, too, that Hans is your son."

"Why not offer him your hand?" said Kathinka.

"So be it," said Micha. He called Hans and Marie to him.
They knelt and received his blessing, and the villagers
joined in a wish for the happiness of the bartered bride
and her bridegroom.

La Gioconda

LA GIOCONDA (The Joyous One) *was composed by Amilcare Ponchielli. Arrigo Boïto wrote the libretto, which he based on a play by Victor Hugo. The opera was first performed in Milan on April 8, 1876.*

ACT I *The Lion's Mouth*

ON A FEAST DAY in Venice crowds had gathered in the courtyard outside the doge's palace. A little apart stood an interested onlooker—Barnaba, chief spy for the Council of Ten that conducted the feared and dreaded Inquisition. Posing as a teller of tales and a singer, he attracted people to him and spied on their actions and conversations.

Bells rang and trumpets sounded, signaling the start of the gondola race. The crowds left the courtyard, shouting, singing, and dancing.

"They dance on their graves," said Barnaba cynically, gesturing toward the gratings of the underground prisons.

La Gioconda, a street singer, came leading her mother into the courtyard. Her mother, La Cieca, was blind. Slowly they moved toward the Church of St. Mark that faced the square.

Barnaba stepped behind a column and secretly watched Gioconda. He was in love with the beautiful street singer.

A wayward butterfly, he called her, and he longed to trap
her in his net.

Gioconda guided her mother to a place near the church.
"Rest here," she said, "while I go to look for the one I love.
I'll return with Enzo."

She started to leave, and Barnaba barred her way. "Enzo
can wait," he said.

"I despise you," she said.

"Wait!—I adore you!" he said, trying to catch her in his
arms. She tore herself away from him and escaped.

Cieca had risen in alarm. "My daughter is in danger,"
she cried. "Her voice—!"

Barnaba laughed contemptuously at the old woman.
When no one answered her call, she felt her way back to
the church steps.

Barnaba watched her, and a thought came to him.
Through this weak old creature he might capture the
daughter.

The gondola race was over. The crowd returned, carrying the winner on their shoulders. Almost unnoticed among
them was Zuàne, one of the losers. Barnaba singled him
out and said, "Suppose I told you why you did not win."

"I know," said Zuàne sullenly. "My boat was over-
weighted."

"Nonsense," said Barnaba. "It was the spell of a sorceress." He indicated Cieca, who sat praying. "I heard her
curse your boat."

Isèpo, a public letter writer, was listening.

"She is in league with the demons," went on Barnaba.
"Blind though she is, she can see you."

Others had drawn near. Already Zuàne believed the old

woman had caused him to lose the race, and the crowd was convinced that she was a heretic who should be burned. The cry went up, "Seize the witch!"

People dragged Cieca into the middle of the courtyard. "Help! I am blind!" she cried. "Have mercy!"

"Take her to prison," said Barnaba, and the crowd began to call for her death.

Gioconda had returned. Enzo was with her. "Murderers!" he shouted, trying to force his way through the crowd to Cieca's side. The people pushed him back, and he rushed off, seeking some of his fellow seamen who would help him rescue Gioconda's mother.

From the doge's palace came Alvise, one of the heads of the Inquisition. With him was Laura, his wife, her face hidden by a mask.

"Rebellion?" said Alvise haughtily. "Does the populace now act as judge and executioner?"

"She is a witch!" said the crowd.

"She is my mother," cried Gioconda.

Laura appealed to her husband, "She is blind, my lord. Spare her life."

Alvise privately consulted Barnaba, asking what the woman had done. Barnaba answered that she was a witch.

Gioconda overheard him. "You lie!" she said. She threw herself at Alvise's feet and pleaded for his mercy.

Enzo came back into the square, bringing a group of Dalmatian sailors. Laura started at the sight of him.

"Be patient," Gioconda told Enzo. "She will be saved."

Barnaba watched Enzo and Laura, trying to read the meaning of the looks that seemed to pass between them.

Laura asked Alvise for permission to remove her mask. He curtly refused, saying he did not wish even the sun to look on her face.

Again Barnaba told Alvise that Cieca was a sorceress.

"She has a rosary," said Laura. "She is a pious woman."

"She is pardoned," said Alvise.

In gratitude Cieca offered her rosary to the one who had saved her—the woman with the angelic voice. Laura accepted the gift and knelt to receive the old woman's blessing. Impatiently her husband pulled her to her feet. He tossed a piece of gold to Gioconda.

She thanked him and asked the name of their benefactress, so that she might remember it in her prayers.

Half-directing the words toward Enzo, Alvise's wife answered that her name was Laura.

"It is she!" exclaimed Enzo.

Alvise led his wife away to the church. Gioconda, too, went toward the church, along with her mother. The crowd followed them.

At the church door Enzo remained behind, while the others went inside. He stood, lost in thought. By now Barnaba had recognized him. Enzo was an exiled prince, banished from Venice as an enemy of the state.

The spy addressed him by name, "Enzo Grimaldo, Prince of Santa Fior, what are you thinking?"

Enzo insisted that he was no prince, but a Dalmatian sailor named Enzo Giordan.

"To all except me," smiled Barnaba. "You are here at the risk of your life. In your native Genoa you loved a maiden, but she became another's bride. That maiden was Laura, wife of Alvise."

Enzo gave up his pretense. All that Barnaba had said was true, he admitted, and now he was promised to Gioconda.

But Barnaba surmised that it was Laura whom Enzo truly loved. "From behind her mask she saw you and knew you," he said. "Tonight Alvise will be at the doge's palace. Laura will be on board your ship."

Enzo was overjoyed. He hurried away.

Barnaba called Isèpo. The letter writer sat down at his desk in the courtyard. Barnaba began to dictate a letter to the secret head of the Inquisition.

Gioconda and Cieca left the church. Gioconda saw Barnaba and drew her mother back out of sight.

Barnaba continued his dictation: "Tonight your wife intends to sail for Dalmatia with Enzo, the seaman, on board his ship."

Gioconda heard the words. In desperation and despair
she went back into the church.

Barnaba took the letter and dismissed Isèpo. He looked
up at the palace, pondering its gloomy and wondrous glory.
There sat the doge in state. Above the doge was the Council
of Ten. Above the Council ruled the king of all—the spy!

To one side of the courtyard was a Lion's Mouth, an
opening made in the wall to receive written accusations.
By this means any citizen could secretly denounce anyone
to the Inquisition. Barnaba placed his letter in the Lion's
Mouth and went away.

Crowds entered and sang and danced in the courtyard.
Vesper prayers began inside the church, and the people
knelt to pray. Gioconda and her mother had come out into
the courtyard. Gioconda was grief-stricken at Enzo's un-
faithfulness, and Cieca tried to comfort her.

ACT II *The Rosary*

That night Enzo's ship lay at anchor off an island in the
lagoon. Sailors moved about on deck, talking and calling to
one another.

Barnaba and Isèpo, dressed as fishermen, came on board.
Within a short time the spy had learned the number of men
and the amount of arms the ship carried. While the sailors
were laughing at one of his jokes, he gave the information
to Isèpo and sent him away.

Barnaba stayed on, talking with the seamen. After a
while he left to meet Laura and bring her to the ship.

Enzo came on deck. He told the sailors to be ready to

sail at his first signal, and he sent them below to rest. Under the night sky he looked out to sea, awaiting Laura's coming.

Barnaba's boat arrived, bringing her to the ship. She came on board, and they greeted each other joyfully, but she warned him that time was flying and they must be watchful.

He went below to give the sailing orders. There was a shrine of the Madonna on deck, and Laura knelt before it. While she was praying, a masked figure came toward her. It was Gioconda, who had been hiding under the prow of the ship.

Laura rose, frightened. "Who are you?" she asked.

"My name is Vengeance," answered Gioconda. "I love the one you love!"

Laura proudly confessed her love for Enzo.

"You shall die," said Gioconda. "I am stronger than you, and my love is stronger!" She raised a dagger, but before

she could strike, she saw in Laura's hand the rosary that had once been Cieca's. Gioconda suddenly remembered that it was to her rival that she owed her mother's life.

She was determined now that Laura should be saved.

Two boatmen had brought Gioconda to the ship and were waiting for her. She called to them. When they brought the boat alongside, she pushed Laura into it, and the boatmen rowed away.

Gioconda went to the other side of the ship for a better view of the departing boat. Barnaba appeared. He had seen the small boat pull away and realized that Laura had escaped.

In the distance he saw Alvise's galley bearing down on Enzo's ship. He tried to point out the small boat to the men on the galley. As he moved out of sight, gesturing wildly, Gioconda returned.

"She is saved," she said to herself. "My mother, how much you have cost me!"

Enzo came up from below. "Laura, where are you?" he asked.

"She has gone," Gioconda told him. "She fled, while I stay. Which of us loves you more?"

"Do not speak of loving me," he said sternly. "It was hate that ruled your hand."

Alvise's galley had drawn near. They heard the roar of cannon.

"You are betrayed," said Gioconda. "Your name was revealed to the Great Council."

Sailors were on deck, ready to try to outrun Alvise's galley. Then it became clear that their way of escape had been cut off.

Enzo vowed that his ship would not be captured. He seized a torch and set fire to the vessel. The flames rose, and he plunged into the sea, crying a last good-by to Laura.

"Always it is Laura," Gioconda said bitterly, "but at least I may die with you!"

ACT III *The House of Gold*

Alvise was alone in a room of his home, the palatial House of Gold. Laura entered, dressed for the ball to be held that night in the adjoining ballroom. "You called me here?" she said.

He greeted her with pretended civility, but soon he became fiercely accusing. Last night she had been able to fly from him, he said. Tonight she was in his grasp.

He laid hands on her and threw her to the floor.

She begged for her life.

"You weep and hope in vain," he said. He parted the draperies at one end of the room, revealing a funeral bier.

A serenade was being sung outside the window. Alvise placed a small flask in Laura's hand. "You must take this poison," he said. "Do you hear that song? Before it has ended, you must be dead."

He left her.

Unseen, Gioconda, who had escaped from Enzo's ship, entered the room. She snatched the poison from Laura and offered her another flask. She had foreseen Laura's danger and had come to save her. The substitute flask, she said, contained a powerful sleeping potion.

"I fear you," said Laura. But time was short. The serenade was ending. She drank the potion and disappeared into the funeral chamber.

Gioconda poured the poison into the empty flask and carried it away with her.

The serenade was over. Alvise returned. On the table he found the flask he had given his wife. It was empty. He looked behind the draperies, then went slowly away.

Once more Gioconda appeared. She, too, looked in at the funeral bier.

"He loves her," she said to herself. For Enzo's sake, Laura must be saved.

In the magnificent ballroom Alvise was welcoming his guests. Gioconda entered, unnoticed. Also mingling with the guests was Enzo. He had escaped from the burning ship, and he had come in disguise to the House of Gold.

Alvise introduced the evening's entertainment—a ballet representing the hours of the day, from dawn to dusk.

The ballet had hardly ended, when there was a disturbance outside. Barnaba came in, dragging Cieca. He had caught the old woman in one of the forbidden rooms, he said.

"I was praying for her, just dead," said Cieca.

A bell tolled, the passing bell that was rung for the dead and dying. Enzo whispered to Barnaba, asking for whom it rang.

"For Laura," answered Barnaba.

Alvise tried to lift the gloom that had fallen over his guests. "If I am gay," he said, "who among you has the right to be sad?"

"I," said Enzo, in an agony of grief. He revealed himself as the exiled Prince of Santa Fior, from whom Alvise had stolen both his country and the woman he loved.

Alvise called for Enzo's arrest.

Cieca denounced Barnaba as a vile and hated spy. "Yesterday you were saved," he said. "Today I'll be revenged."

Gioconda appealed to the spy, trying to bargain for Enzo's life, "Save him, and I am yours." Barnaba promised that he would bring Enzo safely to her.

Alvise addressed his guests: "You shall see how I guard the honor of my name. A woman once brought outrage to me. Behold her now." He drew back a curtain, revealing Laura on the funeral bier.

"Murderer!" cried Enzo. Drawing a dagger, he rushed at Alvise. Guards held him back.

In the confusion Barnaba pushed Cieca out through a secret doorway. Alvise remained near the funeral chamber, gazing in a kind of madness at the motionless figure on the bier.

ACT IV *The Orfano Canal*

Gioconda was alone in a ruined palace on an island in the Orfano Canal. Two men came down the dimly lighted street and knocked at the door. Between them they carried Laura.

Gioconda let them in. She directed them to place Laura on the bed behind a screen, and she offered them the gold she had promised them for bringing the woman to her. The two men were fellow street singers, and they refused payment, saying that true friends willingly helped one another.

She asked them to search for her mother. Last night they had become separated, she said.

After the men had gone she went to the table. A dagger was there, and a flask of poison. With thoughts of suicide, she picked up the flask, then set it down. She asked herself why her rival should not die instead.

Putting the evil thought from her, she began to weep.

Enzo came down the street, found the door open, and entered. It was through Gioconda's help that he had been released from prison, and he thanked her. Yet freedom meant little to him now, and he was determined to end his life.

She asked him, "Would you die for Laura?"

Yes, he answered. He would go to Laura's tomb and die there.

She told him mockingly, "You will find the tomb is empty. I have taken her from it."

Enzo was horrified. "You are lying!"

"No," she said. "I swear it."

He demanded that she explain the mystery. She refused. When he threatened her, she faced him without fear, hoping to die by his hand.

From behind the screen a voice called, "Enzo!"

"Who is there?" he asked.

Laura appeared.

"Enzo, come to me!" she said.

He caught her in his arms. Laura saw Gioconda and said, "It is she who saved my life."

Enzo and Laura knelt in gratitude before Gioconda.

From the direction of the canal came the sound of singing. It was a signal, said Gioconda. The singers were friends, rowing toward the island to carry Enzo and Laura to safety.

A boat drew up outside the palace. Gioconda took off her cloak and put it about Laura's shoulders. She saw on Laura's breast the rosary that had once belonged to Cieca.

"My mother's gift brings you blessing," said Gioconda. Enzo and Laura bade her good-by. They stepped into the boat and were rowed away.

For a little while Gioconda had forgotten her bargain with Barnaba. Now she remembered, and she prayed for guidance and protection.

Barnaba came softly down the street. He stopped outside, watching her through the half-open doorway and listening to her prayer.

Gioconda thought of flight. She ran to the door. Barnaba stopped her.

"This is how you keep a pact?" he asked.

She answered, "I keep the pact."

"Now you are mine!" he said.

"Wait," she said. She began to deck herself out in the imitation jewels and the bright colors she had worn as a ballad singer. All the while she was moving toward the table. When she reached it she grasped the dagger. "I keep my word," she said. "Now I am yours!"

She stabbed herself and fell.

"Hear me and die cursed!" he shouted. "Last night your mother offended me. I strangled her!"

But his revenge had come too late. Gioconda had not heard his words. She was dead.

With a cry of rage and frustration, he fled from the house.

Lakmé

LÉO DELIBES *composed* Lakmé *late in his career. A novel by Pierre Loti suggested the story, and the libretto was written by Edmond Gondinet and Philippe Gille. The opera was first performed in Paris on April 14, 1883.*

ACT I

FOLLOWERS of the Brahmin priest, Nilakantha, met at dawn in his garden sanctuary. Nilakantha had long been scorned and harassed by the British conquerors of India, and he and his people prayed for the downfall of the foreign invaders. Lakmé, his beautiful daughter, joined in the prayer.

The ceremony ended. Alone with his daughter and her two attendants, the priest took leave of Lakmé, telling her he must go to prepare for tomorrow's festival. He left her in the care of the manservant, Hadji, and the maidservant, Mallika.

Hadji went about his duties in the house. Lakmé removed some of her cumbersome jewelry, and she and Mallika rowed off down the stream that flowed near the dwelling.

Trespassers pushed their way through the bamboo paling and into the garden. They were British—two young army

officers, Gerald and Frederic, the governor's daughter, Ellen, her cousin, Rose, and Mrs. Benson, the young ladies' governess.

Gerald and Ellen were sweethearts. To them, exploring the garden was a romantic adventure. Rose, too, found it romantic and amusing. But Mrs. Benson feared they were being imprudent, and Frederic soberly pointed out that they might be placing themselves in danger.

"See the beautiful flowers," said Ellen.

"Don't touch them," Frederic warned her. "They are daturas and deadly poison." He went on to tell the others that this corner of land was inhabited by a fanatical priest and his daughter, Lakmé. The girl's life was dedicated to her religion. She never appeared outside the sanctuary.

In the opinion of Gerald and the Englishwomen this was folly. Women needed admiration and a life of change, they said, but Frederic argued gravely that all women were not the same.

Rose spied the ornaments that Lakmé had left behind. She and Ellen admired their beauty, and Ellen wished for some like them. She asked Gerald to make a sketch of them so that the design could be copied.

"That would be sacrilege," protested Frederic, "and a sacrilege committed here by a European never goes unpunished."

Mrs. Benson insisted on taking her two charges back to the city at once. Frederic accompanied the ladies.

Gerald took out drawing materials, amused at the thought that sketching an ornament could be a serious matter. But the solemn peace of the place began to affect him. Examining the jewels, he tried to picture the girl who wore them.

Suddenly it seemed to him that copying the designs of the jewelry *was* a sacrilege. He was preparing to leave, when Lakmé returned. Quickly he hid behind some bushes.

Lakmé and Mallika placed flowers before the garden shrine. Lakmé suggested that they cool themselves in the

stream, and Mallika went ahead of her into the forest. Before Lakmé could follow, she caught sight of Gerald. She cried out.

At once, Mallika and Hadji were there.

Lakmé pretended that an idle fear had startled her. She sent the servants away, then she went to where Gerald was hiding.

"Your rashness could be punished by death," she said severely.

He was looking at her in rapture.

"If you knew your danger, you would go," she told him.

"Let me look at you," he said.

She was amazed that this strange young man should risk his life to stand and gaze at her.

Her father was returning. She begged Gerald to go.

"I'll not forget you," he said, and he left her.

Nilakantha came into the garden. Hadji came with him and pointed to a break in the bamboo paling.

"Who has profaned this sacred ground?" demanded the priest. A group of Hindus had come into the sanctuary, and they joined Nilakantha in a cry for vengeance.

ACT II

At noon on the day of the festival the city was crowded with people. In the public square Mrs. Benson was pursued by a fortuneteller, a jewel vendor, and a pickpocket. She was threatening them indignantly, when Frederic and Rose heard her voice and came to her rescue.

Gerald and Ellen appeared and stayed to watch the dancing in the square. Frederic had a secret message for Gerald. Their regiment had been ordered out tonight to fight the rebels, he said.

"We must keep this from the ladies," said Gerald, and he conducted Mrs. Benson and Ellen back toward the governor's palace.

Rose and Frederic lingered. She noticed an old man

and a girl, who had been begging in the crowd. The sight of them made her strangely uneasy, she said, and she took Frederic's arm as she walked with him out of the square.

The old man and the girl were Nilakantha and Lakmé. Nilakantha had forced her to accompany him to the festival in disguise. He ordered her to sing in the public square, hoping the enemy intruder would hear her voice and reveal himself.

Lakmé sang, and people gathered to listen. Her father looked about him, muttering, "He has not yet come." He commanded her to repeat the song.

Trembling, she began again. Gerald and Frederic joined the crowd.

"Lakmé!" exclaimed Gerald. "The Brahmin's daughter!"

Nilakantha said in triumph, "The stranger is betrayed!"

Gerald would have gone to her, but Frederic held him back and cautioned him to be prudent.

Military music sounded nearby. "They are calling us," Frederic said, and he led his friend away.

Nilakantha looked after them, saying, "I know him now."

British soldiers marched across the square. Crowds followed them until only Lakmé, Nilakantha, and a group of his followers were left behind. The priest told the others of his plans. They would seek Gerald out and stealthily form a circle around him, then Nilakantha would strike him down. He told his daughter, "Stay here with Hadji."

The servant said, when they were alone, "He thinks only of vengeance. He has not seen your tears. If there is someone you wish to save, give me your command."

Gerald returned, searching for Lakmé. He found her and swore that for her sake he would brave all danger.

Lakmé's father was approaching, and she hurriedly left the square. Gerald, too, went away, as Nilakantha appeared with other Brahmins and a group of sacred dancers. Priests followed in a stately procession.

Mrs. Benson, Ellen, and Rose returned to watch, and Gerald and Frederic joined them. The girls were entertained by the sights and sounds of the festival, but Mrs. Benson complained that everyone had gone mad. Gerald was preoccupied. Frederic told him with good-natured irony that war might have its blessings. "It will keep the one ideal woman from crossing your path!"

He left the group. Brahmins came out of the pagoda that
faced the square. On a palanquin they carried a statue of
the goddess Dourga. Torchbearers accompanied the procession, and the sacred dances were resumed.

Nilakantha and his followers took part in the ceremonies.
The priest was watching Gerald. Gerald's eyes were on
Lakmé, who had come in sight on the edge of the square.
He started toward her.

Nilakantha followed and stabbed him. Gerald fell, and
the priest escaped.

Lakmé ran to Gerald. Her face lighted, as she found
that he was only unconscious, that his wound was not
dangerous. "Now you are mine forever," she said. "May
heaven protect our love!"

ACT III

With the help of the faithful Hadji, Lakmé had brought
Gerald to a hut in the forest. Now she watched over him
while he lay sleeping under a tree that shaded him from
the brilliant sunlight.

He awakened and at first did not see her. Slowly he recalled the festival, the dagger wound, the dark night. She
spoke, telling him it was she who had cared for him. With
her gift of healing, she had healed his wound.

He was ecstatic at being alone with her in this idyllic
setting. Here they would always be together, she said,
hidden away from the world.

A procession of young couples passed nearby. They were

on their way to the holy spring, said Lakmé. According to legend, when two lovers drank of the water from the same cup, their undying love for each other was assured.

Lakmé went to fill a cup at the spring. While she was gone, Frederic appeared. A trail of blood had led him to the hut.

"Lakmé saved me," said Gerald. "Only love could work such a miracle."

Frederic appealed to his friend's reason. Gerald's world and Lakmé's were far apart. "And what of Ellen?" Frederic asked. "What of your duties as a soldier?"

These were questions Gerald had not considered. Their answers recalled him from romance to reality.

Frederic left him. Lakmé came back from the spring carrying a cup of water.

She looked at him tenderly, then, shocked and surprised, she put down the cup. "You are not the same," she said.

He tried to pretend that nothing had changed.

"Do you swear that our lives shall be united?" she asked.

He hesitated, listening to a chorus of soldiers in the distance. She offered him the cup of water, but he did not see it. He was looking in the direction of the voices.

She said to herself, "All is over." She picked a datura blossom and bit it in two.

The song of the soldiers died away. Gerald turned back to Lakmé. He was frightened at the change that had come over her, and he assured her that he was free of the ties of his old life.

"Ah, dearest one, now I believe it," she said. She touched the cup to her lips and handed it to him. He drank from it, pledging that he would belong to her forever.

Nilakantha came upon them. Enraged at the sight of his enemy, he threatened Gerald's life.

"Listen, I pray," said Lakmé. "We have drunk together from the sacred water. If the gods must have a victim, let them claim me."

Nilakantha held her in his arms.

"She is dying," said Gerald, weeping. "It is for me that she is dying."

She spoke her last words to him, "You have given me the fairest dream that anyone could know."

"Ah, beloved!" sobbed Gerald.

But Nilakantha was comforted by the thought that her soul had found eternal life. "Now," he said, "she bears a prayer to heaven."

The Tales of Hoffmann

JACQUES OFFENBACH *composed* The Tales of Hoffmann *to a libretto by Jules Barbier and Michael Carré,
who based their text on several tales of the German poet,
E. T. A. Hoffmann. The opera was first performed in Paris
on February 10, 1881, four months after the composer's
death. By the end of that year* The Tales of Hoffmann *had
had more than a hundred performances.*

PROLOGUE

MOONLIGHT shone through the window of Master
Luther's tavern in Nuremberg. Out of the shadows came
the spirits of beer and wine, who sang their own praises,
then vanished.

Lindorf, a councilor with a strangely evil face, came into
the tavern. Andrès, a servant, entered shortly afterward.
He was employed by Stella, a lovely opera singer. She had
given him a letter to deliver to the poet, Hoffmann.

Lindorf admired Stella and was jealous of her attentions
to anyone else. He bribed the servant to give up the letter,
which he opened as soon as Andrès had gone.

Stella had written that she was sorry for having hurt
Hoffmann's feelings. Enclosed with the letter was the key
to her dressing room at the theater. "If you love me," she
wrote, "you can find me there."

Master Luther brought his waiters into the tavern. Students began to arrive, among them Nathanael and Hermann. Nathanael proposed a toast to Stella, and after they had drunk, the students began to ask for their friend, Hoffmann.

"Gentlemen, he is here," said Luther, and Hoffmann entered with his faithful companion, Nicklausse.

Hoffmann was gloomy and absorbed in his own thoughts. Nathanael asked him to sing. The poet obliged with a wry little song about a dwarf named Klein-Zach. But when he began to describe the dwarf's features, his thoughts wandered. He described instead a beautiful woman.

Luther lighted the punch bowl, and the students sang a humorous and satirical song to him.

Hoffmann and Lindorf exchanged a few barbed words. Hoffmann told the others that Lindorf constantly brought him ill-luck, not only at cards, but in love.

"So you are sometimes in love?" said Lindorf.

Hoffmann replied that he loved Stella, who was three women in one, a combination of the three enchantresses who had shared his life. "Shall I tell you the story of my loves?" he asked.

"Yes!" said the others, and they settled back to listen.

Hoffmann began, "The name of the first was Olympia."

ACT I *Olympia*

Hoffmann had come to the home of Spalanzani, a scientist and inventor. While he waited alone he looked at the curtain across one end of the room. "She is there," he said to himself. "If I dared—"

He lifted the curtain and gazed at the figure of a girl, who seemed to be sleeping.

"How beautiful she is!" he said.

Nicklausse entered. Hoffmann spoke of his love for Olympia.

"Does she know of your love?" asked Nicklausse.

Hoffmann admitted that she did not.

"Speak to her," said Nicklausse.

"I dare not," said Hoffmann.

"Then sing," said Nicklausse.

"Spalanzani doesn't like music," said Hoffmann.

Nicklausse laughed. "I know. Everything for science,"

he said, and he sang a song about a mechanical doll and a
brass cock and how the two danced and talked together.

Spalanzani led a group of invited guests into the room.
In a moment, he told them, they would be satisfied, and he
and his servant, Cochenille, went out together.

Nicklausse said to Hoffmann, "Now we shall have a
closer view of this marvel."

"Silence," said Hoffmann. "Here she is."

Spalanzani had returned, bringing Olympia. He introduced her as his daughter. The guests admired her eyes,
her figure, her clothes, and they agreed that she was indeed
ravishing.

Cochenille brought out a harp, and Olympia sang to
Spalanzani's accompaniment.

Supper was announced. Spalanzani asked a favor of Hoffmann. Olympia was a bit tired, he said. Would Hoffmann stay with her?

"Oh, happiness!" said Hoffmann.

Alone with Olympia, he told her of his admiration for her. "Let me gaze on your charming face," he said.

He touched her shoulder. "Yes," she said.

"I thought I heard you sigh," he said, again touching her shoulder.

"Yes," she said.

To Hoffmann this was an avowal of love. "You are mine," he declared. "Our hearts are forever united." He pressed her hand. She rose, walked up and down, then left the room.

He was bewildered. "You do not answer," he said. "Speak! Have I wounded you?" He started after her. Nicklausse came in and stopped him.

Hoffmann said wildly, "I am beloved by her!"

"If you knew what they are saying of your loved one—" began Nicklausse.

"What can they say?" asked Hoffmann.

"That she is dead," said Nicklausse, "or never was alive."

But the infatuated Hoffmann could only repeat, "I am beloved by her." He went out to find Olympia, and Nicklausse followed.

Coppélius, another scientist and inventor, came storming in. He was furious, claiming that Spalanzani had swindled him. He swore to be revenged, and he slipped into the next room.

Spalanzani, Olympia, and all the guests returned. The dancing began. Hoffmann waltzed with Olympia. They danced out through one doorway and in through another. She had quickened the pace until he was dizzy and exhausted. Spalanzani stopped them, and Hoffmann fell into a chair.

"Enough, my child," said Spalanzani.

"Yes," said Olympia.

Cochenille gave her a push toward her room. She disappeared, with a peal of metallic laughter.

Hoffmann was still slumped in the chair. Nicklausse and Spalanzani tried to revive him.

Cochenille went to Spalanzani and agitatedly told him that a man was in Olympia's room.

From the next room came a crash of breaking springs.

"She is broken!" cried Spalanzani.

"Broken?" repeated Hoffmann. He ran out, as Coppélius came in. "Yes, smashed!" said the rival inventor, with a diabolical laugh.

"Rascal!" shouted Spalanzani. He and Coppélius threw themselves at each other.

Hoffmann returned. He was stricken and pale. His beloved Olympia had been nothing more than a mechanical doll put together by the two scientists, who had hoped to realize a profit on their invention.

"He loved an automaton! An automaton!" jeered the guests, and they laughed at Hoffmann's despair.

ACT II *Giulietta*

Giulietta, a wealthy woman of Venice, was entertaining Hoffmann, Nicklausse, and other guests in her palace overlooking the Grand Canal. She and Nicklausse were outside, singing a romantic barcarolle to the beauty of the night. When they came inside, Hoffmann declared that such languishing sentiments were not for him. He sang a song that praised the pleasures of music and wine.

Schlemil and Pitichinaccio, two of Giulietta's admirers, exchanged sharp words. She tried to calm them.

As she started toward the card tables, Hoffmann offered her his arm, and the jealous Schlemil thrust himself between them. "To the game, gentlemen," she said, and they all went out except Nicklausse and Hoffmann.

Nicklausse was anxious for his friend's safety. "I have two horses saddled," he said. "At the first dream you permit yourself, I carry you off."

Hoffmann asked what dream there could be. Did one love such a woman as Giulietta?

Nicklausse pointed out that Schlemil seemed to be mad about her.

"I am not Schlemil," said Hoffmann with finality, and they went out.

Dapertutto, a sorcerer, had come into the room in time to overhear part of the conversation. "The eyes of Giulietta are a sure weapon," he said to himself. He took a ring from his finger—a ring set with a large, sparkling diamond.

Giulietta appeared, saw the diamond, and moved toward it as if in fascination. He placed the ring on her finger. She asked, "What do you wish of your servant?"

"You have given me Schlemil's shadow," he said. "Now I pray you to get for me the reflection of Hoffmann." He suggested that this might be too difficult a task for her. "I was listening a while ago," he said, "and he defies you."

Giulietta accepted the challenge. "He shall be my toy," she promised.

As Dapertutto went out, Hoffmann entered. Not caring to be alone with Giulietta, he, too, started to leave, but she detained him. Hoffmann ironically remarked that there was no reason for him to stay—he had lost all his money at cards.

"Ah, you wrong me," she reproached him. With tears in her eyes, she began to weave her spell about him.

Quickly he was caught in her enchantment, believing himself in love with her. She warned him that her love might cost him his life and told him he must go at once. "Strengthen my courage by leaving me something of you," she said.

"What do you want?" he asked.

She asked for his reflection. "It can detach itself from the polished glass and come to hide in my heart," she said.

Her request left him fearful yet delighted. Looking into the mirror she held for him, he promised her his image, his life, his soul.

"Dear one, give them to me," she said.

Suddenly Schlemil was there, along with Nicklausse, Dapertutto, Pitichinaccio, and the other guests.

"Gentlemen, it seems we have been abandoned for Hoffmann," said Schlemil.

Giulietta whispered to Hoffmann, "I love you." She added that Schlemil had a key that belonged to her.

Pitichinaccio said to Schlemil, "Let us kill him."

"Patience," said Schlemil.

"How pale you are," Dapertutto said to Hoffmann, and he held up a mirror. Hoffmann looked into it and was amazed. His reflection was gone.

"Ladies, gentlemen, here are the gondolas," said Giulietta. "It is the hour of farewells." She went away.

Nicklausse asked Hoffmann to leave with him.

"Not yet," said Hoffmann, and Nicklausse went outside to wait for him.

Schlemil asked the poet why he stayed behind.

"To get from you a certain key," answered Hoffmann.

"You shall have it only with my life," replied Schlemil.

Dapertutto said to Hoffmann, "You have no sword. Take mine."

Hoffmann took the weapon. He and Schlemil fought, and Schlemil fell, mortally wounded. Hoffmann took the key from him and ran to Giulietta's room, where he had supposed she would be waiting. No one was there.

He came back, and from a gallery overlooking the canal he saw Giulietta in a gondola. She was laughing at him.

Dapertutto called to her, "What will you do with him now?"

She said, "I leave him to you."

Pitichinaccio was in the gondola with Giulietta. "Dear angel!" he said. She took him in her arms, and they drifted away, accompanied by the tender music of the barcarolle.

Now Hoffmann realized how she had deceived him. "Vile wretch!" he shouted after her.

Nicklausse returned. "The police!" he said. The death of Schlemil had been discovered. Nicklausse dragged Hoffmann away.

ACT III *Antonia*

Antonia, a beautiful young singer, was alone in the music
room of her father's house in Munich. On one wall was the
portrait of a woman. The other walls were hung with
violins.

The girl was playing the clavichord and singing a sad

little song. Crespel, her father, entered and reproached her, "Unhappy child, you promised you would sing no more."

Antonia answered that while she sang she fancied she was hearing her mother. But she promised never to sing again, and went sadly away.

Crespel was in despair. He had seen the mark of the malady from which she was suffering—an unnatural color in her cheeks. Singing exhausted her and aggravated her illness. Crespel feared he would lose her as he had lost her mother. "Ah, that Hoffmann!" he said. "It is he who put this madness into her heart."

He had brought his daughter to Munich to escape the poet. He called his servant, Franz, and instructed him to let no one into the house. Franz, as usual, misunderstood, and Crespel stalked off, exasperated at the servant's stupidity.

Franz complained of his master's irritation and commended himself for his cheerfulness and his hidden talents, which were singing and dancing. But when he tried a dance step, he stumbled and fell.

He was picking himself up, when Hoffmann and Nicklausse entered. Hoffmann asked for Antonia.

Franz went out, and presently Antonia came running into the room. Hoffmann took her in his arms, and Nicklausse quietly disappeared.

"I knew you loved me," said Antonia.

"But why were we separated?" asked Hoffmann.

Antonia did not know.

"Tomorrow you shall be my wife," said Hoffmann, and he playfully confessed that he was jealous of music because she loved it so much.

She smiled at this fancy. "Surely you will not forbid me to sing, as my father did," she said.

"What are you saying?" he said in surprise.

"Yes, my father imposes upon me the virtue of silence," she said, but she made it plain that she had no intention of obeying him. She drew Hoffmann to the clavichord and began a love song they had sung together. He sang with her. Suddenly she put her hand to her heart and seemed about to faint. He was alarmed, but she insisted there was nothing the matter.

They heard steps outside.

"My father!" she said. She ran out. Hoffmann stayed and hid himself in a window recess, with an idea of finding the solution of the mystery surrounding Antonia.

Crespel entered. He had thought Hoffmann was there, but when he looked about, he saw no one.

The servant came in and announced Doctor Miracle.

"That scoundrel—gravedigger—assassin!" said Crespel. "Drive him away!"

The sinister figure of Doctor Miracle appeared, and the servant fled. With a hideous geniality, Miracle inquired about Antonia. "Dear girl, we'll cure her," he said. "Take me to her."

Crespel threatened to throw him out of the house.

"Softly!" said Miracle. "I don't wish to displease you." He began making hypnotic gestures toward Antonia's room. Crespel was horrified, and Hoffmann, too, watched in horror, as the door of the girl's room slowly opened. Miracle spoke, as if to an invisible Antonia. He went through the motions of leading her to a chair. He asked her questions and told her to sing.

"No, don't have her sing!" said Crespel.

"Her face brightens, her eyes burn, she carries her hand to her heart," said Miracle. His gaze seemed to follow her invisible figure back across the room. The door closed.

Miracle took some medicine vials from his pocket and rattled them together like castanets. He urged Crespel to accept his aid.

"Be off!" said Crespel, and he pushed Miracle out of the house.

Miracle reappeared, walking through the wall and continuing to urge his course of treatment for Antonia.

"Away!" shouted Crespel, and he and Miracle disappeared together.

Hoffmann came out of the window recess. Now he understood something of Antonia's illness and why she must not sing again.

Antonia returned. "What did my father say?" she asked.

Hoffmann refused to tell her, but he asked her to give up all thought of singing and all her dreams of future success and glory. She agreed to do as he asked, and he took leave of her.

"He has become the ally of my father," she said to herself. "But I promised. I shall sing no more."

Doctor Miracle appeared behind her. "You will sing no more?" he said. "Do you know what a sacrifice he imposes on your youth?" Must all her talent be abandoned for the life of a middle-class housewife? Did she not realize that Hoffmann cared only for her beauty and when it was gone, he would no longer be faithful?

Miracle disappeared.

"I've sworn to be Hoffmann's," said Antonia. "I may not take back my word. My mother, my mother, I love him!"

Again Doctor Miracle was there. "Your mother?" he said. "Do you not know she speaks through me?"

The portrait on the wall began to move and glow. A spirit voice spoke, "Dear child, it is your mother."

"Do you hear?" said Miracle. "It is the voice of your best counselor."

The spirit and Antonia called to each other.

"She seems to live again. The applause of the crowd fills her with joy!" said Miracle. "Join with her!"

He seized a violin and played furiously, goading Antonia on, until she began to sing with the spirit voice. The song rose to a frenzied climax, and Antonia fell, dying.

With a burst of laughter, Miracle disappeared. Crespel came running in. "My mother calls me," said Antonia with her dying breath.

The father's grief-stricken cries brought Hoffmann. Crespel turned on him accusingly. "It is you who killed her!" he said, and he attacked Hoffmann with a knife. Nicklausse was there in time to intervene.

"Quick! A doctor!" said Hoffmann.

"Here," said a voice, and Doctor Miracle appeared. He bent over Antonia and pronounced her dead.

"My child, my daughter!" sobbed Crespel.

"Antonia!" cried Hoffmann.

EPILOGUE

The three tales were finished. "There is the story of my loves," Hoffmann said to the listeners in Luther's tavern. "The memory will always remain in my heart."

The student, Nathanael, was puzzled by the tales, but Nicklausse understood their meaning. The stories were three dramas in one, he said. Olympia, Giulietta, and Antonia were three women in one. They were all—Stella.

Hoffmann had put Stella out of his thoughts. He wanted only to drink himself into oblivion.

Again the students sang their drinking song. Then, along with Nicklausse, Master Luther, and Lindorf, they trooped out of the tavern.

In an aureole of light the Muse appeared. She spoke to

Hoffmann: "Am I nothing to you? I love you. Be mine. I will ease your sufferings. One is great by love, but greater by tears."

She vanished. In ecstasy he gave himself up to the Muse, knowing that only as a poet would he find peace.

Stella came into the tavern. Nicklausse was with her. The students followed.

Stella looked at Hoffmann. "Asleep," she said.

"No, drunk," said Nicklausse.

Lindorf entered. Stella took his arm, and they moved toward the door. Then she paused and threw a flower at Hoffmann's feet. He gazed after her in a stupor, as she went out with Lindorf.

Samson and Delilah

SAMSON AND DELILAH *is the best known of the twelve operas by Camille Saint-Saëns. The libretto, by Ferdinand Lemaire, is based on the Biblical story. Paris opera companies would not produce the work because they believed it could never be a popular success. Through the influence of the composer-pianist, Franz Liszt,* Samson and Delilah *was taken to Germany and first performed there—in Weimar—on December 2, 1877. The opera was acclaimed, although it was not heard in Paris until thirteen years later.*

ACT I

THRONGS OF HEBREWS had gathered in the city of Gaza, in ancient Palestine. Their nation had been conquered, their cities destroyed, their altars profaned. They cried out that God had forsaken them.

From among them came Samson, a man of great courage and physical strength. "Pause, O my brethren," he said. "In my heart the voice of the Lord speaks words of hope. We shall be free and once more raise our altars."

The others continued to lament that God no longer heeded their prayers.

He turned on them, angry that they should doubt the Lord's mercy. "Wretched souls, keep silent!" he said. "God

reigns above you. He will strengthen your arm and endow you with might."

The others began to take courage, believing Samson's words were from the Lord.

Abimelech, ruler of Gaza, entered at the head of his Philistine warriors. "Who dares to raise his voice?" he said. "Your prayer is vain. We are your conquerors forever," and he heaped scorn on the Hebrews.

Samson cried out to God, "Let the earth tremble beneath him. Let the enemy fly with fear before the Lord's vengeance."

The other Hebrews took up the cry.

Abimelech drew his sword and attacked Samson. Samson wrested the weapon from him and stabbed him with it. Abimelech fell. Philistines ran to his aid, and Samson held them back with Abimelech's sword. In the confusion, the Hebrews fled, and Samson escaped with them.

Near-by was the temple of Dagon, the Philistines' god. The high priest came out of the temple, followed by attendants and guards. Standing beside the body of Abimelech, he commanded the warriors to make haste and avenge their prince.

But the warriors were frightened. Before Samson's might they had seemed powerless.

A messenger brought word that the Hebrews were in revolt. The high priest cursed Samson and his followers, and the Philistines fled toward the distant mountains.

The Hebrews returned in triumph to Gaza, and when Samson appeared, they hailed him as their mighty leader.

Delilah, a priestess of Dagon, came out of the temple. Behind her came a procession of Philistine women carrying garlands of flowers. They welcomed the Hebrews, and Delilah invited Samson to come with her to the fair valley of Sorek.

He tried to close his eyes and heart to her beauty, and an old Hebrew man warned him against her charms.

Philistine maidens danced for the pleasure of the Hebrew warriors. Delilah joined in the dance, glancing from time

to time at Samson. In vain he tried to avoid her eyes, and he listened raptly to the song she sang of love and springtime.

Again the old Hebrew man warned Samson to shun her evil powers, as Delilah continued her song from the steps of the temple.

ACT II

Dusk had come to the valley of Sorek. Delilah, richly dressed, sat near the doorway of her dwelling, waiting for Samson. The high priest found her there. He spoke of the Hebrew revolt and the disaster Samson had brought to the Philistines.

"But his strength vanished that day at the feet of Delilah," said the priest. "Use your powers, take him captive, and you shall be paid any ransom you may ask."

She answered that she sought no ransom. "More than you, I detest him," she said. Three times she had asked him the secret of his strength. Three times he had deceived her, but tonight she was resolved to bring all her charms to bear and learn the truth.

The priest left her, promising that he would soon return. Delilah went slowly to the entrance of her house and stood waiting. In spite of herself she had begun to doubt her powers.

Samson appeared outside the house. Once more he had been drawn there against his will.

Delilah greeted him, calling him her own and her best beloved. Samson was hesitant and troubled. He was pledged to his own God and his own people, he told her, and he must bid her farewell.

She wept. With tears and pleading she drew from him a confession of his love for her.

If he truly loved her, she said, he would reveal the secret he had kept hidden from her.

"Leave me!" he cried.

"Tell me!" she insisted.

"Do not ask me," he said.

She turned from him. "There is no love in your heart," she said. "I despise you!"

She ran into the house.

A storm was breaking. Samson raised his arms, as if appealing to heaven. Then he hurried after Delilah.

Philistine soldiers approached the house. The storm continued, and there was a violent crash of thunder.

Delilah came to the doorway. "Philistines—your aid!" she called.

From within, Samson cried in anguish, "I am betrayed!" and the soldiers rushed into the house.

ACT III

Samson, in chains, was turning a grinding-mill in the prison at Gaza. He had been blinded. His hair, once the secret source of his strength, had been shorn by Delilah.

He prayed to the Lord for mercy. Hebrews in another part of the prison reproached him for having broken his promises, and he offered his life to God in atonement. Philistine soldiers came into the prison and took him away.

Inside the temple of Dagon the high priest stood surrounded by Philistines. Delilah entered with a procession of young women. Day was dawning, and the Philistines sang and danced to greet the sun.

A child led Samson into the temple.

"Hail, judge of Israel, who, by his presence, makes our festival the more splendid," said the high priest, and he mockingly invited Samson to drink to Delilah.

The priestess went near Samson. "Now Delilah's vengeance comes," she said.

The high priest taunted Samson, "Let Jehovah show his might and cure your blindness."

"Do you permit this, my God!" cried Samson. "Hear me—make me victorious!"

The Philistines laughed and jeered at his helplessness.

Delilah and the high priest performed a ceremonial rite to the god Dagon. A victim was to be offered on the sacrificial altar. "Come, Samson," said the priest. "Come, please our god." He spoke to the child who had led Samson into the temple. "Guide him where all may see him."

"Be with me, O Lord. Inspire me with your might," prayed Samson. He said softly to the child, "Take me to the marble pillars." The child led him to a place between the two great columns that supported the temple. The Philistines were singing, "Glory to Dagon, glory, glory!"

Samson stretched out his arms so that his hands were on the pillars. "Lord, remember me," he prayed fervently. "One moment make me strong!"

With a great effort he toppled the pillars. Amid the shrieks of the people, the temple collapsed in ruins, destroying everyone gathered beneath the roof.

Boris Godunoff

MODEST MOUSSORGSKY *wrote both the libretto and music of* Boris Godunoff. *The story is from a drama by Pushkin. At its first performance—in St. Petersburg, on February 8, 1874—the opera was a success with the public, although the critics were late in recognizing its greatness.*

PROLOGUE

TOWARD THE END of the sixteenth century young Dmitri, heir to the Russian throne, was murdered. Seven years later the tsar died, leaving the throne vacant.

Boris Godunoff, brother-in-law of the tsar, had retired to a monastery near Moscow. Now there were crowds of peasants outside the monastery. They had been assembled to take part in a demonstration arranged by Russian nobles, who wished to place Boris on the throne.

Prince Schouïsky, Boris' adviser, entered the monastery with a group of nobles. A police officer brandished a stick and commanded the peasants to make the demonstration more realistic.

Hardly understanding the situation, they obediently dropped to their knees, droning the words they had been taught, "Why do you abandon us? See us weeping—hear our sobs! Mercy, good father!"

Tchelkaloff, secretary of the parliament, came out of the monastery and sadly told the crowds that Boris had refused the throne. "Our land suffers and laments," he said. "Pray that he may grant the favor we seek."

Pilgrims mingled with the peasants, handed out sacred images, then advanced toward the monastery, while Boris held himself aloof, pretending to be unmoved by the pleas of the populace.

But word soon spread across the land that Boris had at last yielded to the wishes of the people. In the square of the Kremlin great crowds gathered for the coronation. Bells rang. A procession wound through the square and into the Cathedral of the Assumption.

Boris appeared. His son, Feodor, and his daughter, Xenia, were with him. In his heart were fears and presentiments of evil, as he prayed that his reign might be just and happy.

"Let us salute the dead sovereign of Russia," he said. "Then all the people shall have their feast. The tsar invites you."

He disappeared into the cathedral. The people acclaimed him with wild enthusiasm, and bells tolled throughout the city.

ACT I

Five years had passed since Boris' coronation. Pimenn, a monk, sat writing in a cell in the Monastery of the Miracle. Grigori, a novice, lay sleeping nearby. Pimenn was setting down the events he had witnessed, so that future genera-

tions might learn the history of the past. In another part of the monastery monks were praying. From time to time their voices could be heard in the cell.

Grigori woke from a nightmare. He told Pimenn his dream. "I saw all Moscow at my feet. The crowd below pointed to me, with jeering laughter. In shame and terror, I fell . . . and woke."

"Calm yourself with prayer," said Pimenn. "If I sleep without having prayed, fights and battles and follies of my youth rise before me, and my rest is lost."

Grigori envied the older man his youthful adventures. "You saw Ivan the Terrible in splendor, while I have spent my life as an humble monk."

"Do not lament," said Pimenn. He named tsars who had exchanged their worldly glory for the peace and rest of a monastery. One of these was the pious ruler who had preceded Boris. "Never more shall we have such a tsar," he said. "Heaven has punished us. Now an infamous murderer rules the land."

Grigori spoke of the murdered Dmitri, who would have inherited the throne if he had lived. "How old would he be now?" he asked.

"He would be your age," said Pimenn. Before the night was over, he said, he would end his chronicles with the horrible crime of the present tsar.

He left the cell. "Boris! Boris!" exclaimed Grigori. "All bow down before you. No one would dare remind you of that boy's sad fate. But here in this cell is one who has recorded your blackness. The justice of men shall strike you, and God will also judge!"

*

In a tavern near the Lithuanian border the hostess sat singing. Voices interrupted her song. She opened the door and admitted two men, Varlaam and Missaïl, in the garb of holy hermits. Another man followed them. He was Grigori, dressed as a peasant.

Varlaam and Missaïl, who were vagabonds posing as holy men, had met Grigori on the road. They knew little about him and looked on him with some suspicion.

The hostess served wine. While his two companions drank, Grigori asked the way to the Lithuanian border. It was not far, the hostess told him, but she warned him that the police were on the trail of someone and all travelers were stopped at the border.

"Do you know whom they seek?" he asked.

The hostess was not sure. Perhaps a robber, she said, but she doubted that the police would catch him. There was an unguarded road by which anyone could escape into Lithuania. She carefully explained to him how the byway could be found.

There was a knock at the door. Soldiers entered, and the captain began to question the men.

Varlaam and Missaïl insisted that they were poor churchmen gathering alms.

"And who are you?" the captain asked Grigori.

He answered that he lived nearby and was traveling with the hermits as far as the border.

The captain produced a warrant for the arrest of an escaped heretic. "The tsar orders him taken dead or alive," he said. He thrust the paper out at Varlaam.

"Why give it to me?" asked Varlaam.

"Because you are the heretic," said the captain.

"It is a mistake!" cried Varlaam.

"Which of you can read?" asked the officer.

Grigori came forward. The captain handed him the warrant and ordered him to read it aloud.

Grigori began. It was a warrant for his own arrest. " 'A worthless novice, Grigori, has escaped from the monastery . . . tempted by the evil spirit, he sought to bring trouble on his brothers . . . . The tsar orders that he be arrested—' "

". . . and hanged," said the captain.

"It does not say so here," said Grigori.

"You lie," said the captain.

Grigori had surmised by now that the captain could not read. He came to the description of the wanted man, but instead of reading it, he substituted a description of Varlaam: "Age fifty years . . . beard white . . . round of paunch . . . a red nose . . . ."

"This is the man," said the captain, and the soldiers fell upon Varlaam. He fought them off. "These are lies," he protested. "Even though I can scarcely read, I know the letters, and because of the gallows, I *will* read!" He seized the warrant. Haltingly he spelled out the description of the escaped man: " 'His age twenty years . . . of middle height . . . reddish hair . . . on the nose a wart . . . .' " He pointed to Grigori. "It is you!"

"It is he!" said the soldiers.

But before they could lay hands on him, Grigori had leaped through the window and was gone.

ACT II

Feodor and Xenia, Boris' son and daughter, sat with an old nurse in the apartments of the tsar. Xenia was weeping over a portrait of her dead sweetheart. The nurse tried to console her by singing a song. Young Feodor began a song of his own, and he and the nurse sang and played a game together, but the old woman stopped fearfully as Boris entered.

"Am I a hawk come to threaten the young ones?" he asked.

"My lord, forgive me," she said. "I am an old woman and easily frightened."

Boris spoke comfortingly to his daughter and sent her and the nurse away. He looked at the atlas his son had been reading. Feodor pointed out a map in the book that showed the entire empire.

"Study it well," said Boris. "Some day—perhaps soon—all this may belong to you." He turned away, reflecting on the years of his reign, years with neither joy nor peace. He had hoped to make a happy marriage for his daughter, but her lover had died. The land had been swept by pestilence and famine. From all sides came rumors of plots against him. And at night visions of the murdered boy, Dmitri, came to haunt him.

There were loud voices in the next room. Boris sent Feodor to see what was happening.

A nobleman entered. He whispered the news that other nobles, including Schouïsky, were plotting against the tsar. "A messenger has arrived from Cracow—" he began.

"Arrest him!" said Boris, and the nobleman hurried out.

Feodor came back and gave a long and detailed account of what had caused the excitement outside. The nurses had teased the parrot. The parrot, in turn, had tried to bite them.

Boris held the boy on his knees, and said with deep feeling, "With what grace and frankness you have told your simple story! I can see your wisdom and the fruits of your learning. Oh, if only I could know the joy of seeing you wisely rule as Russia's tsar!"

Prince Schouïsky entered with more disturbing news. The messenger from Cracow had been arrested and had revealed that an imposter was claiming to be the tsar.

"Under what name does the traitor hide?" asked Boris. Schouïsky answered that the man called himself Dmitri.

"Dmitri!" repeated Boris in horror. He led his son out of the room and came back to Schouïsky. "See to it that all the realm is guarded," he said, and he asked, "Have you ever heard that murdered boys rise from their graves to vex the souls of tsars?" He burst into wild laughter, then he asked anxiously for assurance that the boy who had perished was really Dmitri.

Schouïsky replied that Dmitri was certainly in his tomb.

Boris remained shaken and fearful. He sent Schouïsky away, and when he was alone, he gave way to terror and an agony of guilt.

The room darkened. The clock struck. Boris seemed to see the figure of Dmitri moving toward him. "Go away!" he cried. "I am not the murderer! No, boy, not I. It was the people!"

With his face in his hands, he dropped to his knees and prayed, "O Lord, protect the guilty soul of Boris!"

ACT III

In her father's castle in Poland the Princess Marina sat idly listening while attendants sang a song praising her loveliness. Their flattery wearied her. She much preferred patriotic songs of Polish heroes, she said, and she sent the attendants away.

She thought of the young man she had lately met. "My Dmitri," she called him. She was sure that heaven had sent him to overthrow the evil Boris, and she pictured herself beside Dmitri on the throne of Russia.

Rangoni, a Jesuit monk, entered. The holy church was in a state of neglect, he said, and it was her duty to convert the people of Moscow.

She answered that she was not worthy of such a mission. He persisted, telling her how to capture the young man from Moscow with soft words and tender glances. Then, when he was her slave, she must make him swear to take up the cause of the church.

She was repelled by his treachery and deceit. She refused to obey him.

He angrily upbraided her, telling her that for the holy cause she must be willing to make any sacrifice.

Aroused in turn, she ordered him out of her sight.

"A flame devours you, your lips are distorted, your color is ghastly," he said. "All your beauty is vanishing, dispelled by the Evil One!"

She trembled in fear. She begged for mercy.

"Believe in me," said the monk. "Obey me in all things."

Grigori, the false Dmitri, had come to the castle of Marina's father. "Meet me tonight at the fountain," the princess had said, and he waited impatiently in the garden.

Rangoni appeared. "Marina has sent me," he said. "She wishes you to know that she loves you and will come to you." He warned the young man to protect himself from those who surrounded the princess.

Inside the castle an orchestra struck up a polonaise. Marina and her guests came through the garden. Rangoni disappeared, and Grigori hid among the trees. The princess was on the arm of an old Polish nobleman. "Your vows of love leave me indifferent," she told him coldly, as they passed by.

She and her guests returned to the castle. Grigori had seen Marina and the nobleman together. While he waited, torn by jealousy and doubt, she called to him.

"My queen, my angel of beauty!" he cried, as she came back into the garden.

"I am here to speak of grave things, but not of love," she said. "When will you enter Moscow as tsar?"

He was afraid, he told her. He feared that her longing for glory had left her incapable of love.

She scorned him for languishing in his dreams of love and forgetting Boris and the crown of Russia. "Worthless one," she said. "Leave me!"

He was stung by her cruelty. "I am tsar!" he said furiously. "Tomorrow at dawn I lead my troops to battle. And from my throne in the Kremlin I'll see you there imploring, but everyone shall laugh at the foolish lady of Poland!"

At once she asked his forgiveness. "It was not hate that inspired my words," she said, "but my belief in your destiny. I wish glory and power for you. But forget my love a while and make haste to seize your throne."

She knelt before him. He lifted her and took her in his arms. In the shadows Rangoni watched and enjoyed his triumph.

ACT IV

At night, near the Russian town of Kromy, a crowd of vagabonds rushed into a forest clearing. They had captured a nobleman, Kroutschov, and were dragging him with them.

They gagged their prisoner and tied him to the trunk of a fallen tree. Two men posed on either side of him, pretending to be his escort. To make further mockery of him, they placed a mumbling, coughing old woman beside him, saying their noble guest must have a sweetheart.

The village simpleton came into the clearing. He wore a tin helmet, his clothes were ragged, and his feet were bare. Boys ran after him, laughing and calling him Old Saucepan-Hat.

Hardly noticing them, he sat down on a stone and began to sing, swaying from side to side. The boys stood about him, striking his helmet and pretending it was a bell. Innocently he told them he had a kopeck. When he showed them the coin they took it from him and ran away, and he wept, crying that he had been robbed.

Varlaam and Missaïl came into the clearing. They urged the crowd of peasants to rise against Boris and accept Dmitri as their rightful tsar.

Two Jesuit priests, Lovitzki and Tcherniakovski, approached, singing a hymn.

"Vile scavengers!" said Varlaam and Missaïl. "Here they come, like us, to acclaim Dmitri. We must stop them."

Missaïl shouted, "Death to the black brood!" and the mob fell upon the Jesuits and dragged them into the forest.

Armed men began to appear—troops of Grigori, the false

Dmitri. Grigori himself entered on horseback, and the crowd hailed him. Kroutschov, who had been unbound and ungagged, bowed low and called out, "Glory to you, gracious tsar!"

"Rise and follow us to Moscow," said Grigori. "Let us seek the Kremlin."

Kroutschov followed, along with the vagabonds and the two priests, who had been released.

Bells rang, the glow of distant fires lighted the sky. Only the simpleton was left in the clearing. Sitting on a stone, he swayed from side to side and sang, "Flow, flow, my bitter tears . . . . The enemy shall come, and the world shall grow dark. Woe and sorrow always. Weep, Russian folk, poor hungry folk."

Noblemen had met in the tsar's palace for a special session of the royal council. They spoke in judgment of the false Dmitri, who sought to usurp the throne. Dire punishments were proposed, but some of the men reminded the others, "Before your hare is roasted, he must be caught."

Schouïsky arrived. He said to the nobles who surrounded him that he feared for Boris' sanity. "I saw him pale and trembling," he said. "He seemed to see some terrible spectre, and he spoke to it, saying, 'Go, go, boy, go!' "

The nobles doubted his word.

Boris entered, staring wildly into space. "Go, go, go, boy!" he said.

Silently the nobles watched and listened.

"I the murderer? No, no," said Boris.

Then, gaining control of himself, he took the seat reserved for him. With a lordly manner, he addressed the nobles, "I bade you meet, for I need your counsel in these threatening times."

Schouïsky spoke. "An old man waits to see you. He has some mystery to disclose to you."

The old monk, Pimenn, was admitted. He told the story of a blind shepherd to whom the voice of the child, Dmitri, had spoken in a dream: "Visit the cathedral and pray at my tomb. God has numbered me among his saints, to work my miracles." The shepherd had prayed at the tomb and his eyesight had been miraculously restored.

Boris was overcome with emotion. He fell unconscious, and some of the nobles caught him in their arms. When he had revived he called for his son and sent everyone else away.

Feodor entered. The others left the father and son alone together.

Boris bade Feodor farewell. "Soon you shall rule," he said. "Do not seek to learn how I gained the throne. You are not accountable. Rule justly, defend the holy church, and protect my Xenia."

A funeral bell was tolling. From outside came voices, "Weep, all . . . his life is passing."

Feodor, weeping, said, "My father, calm yourself. The Lord will help you."

"No, my son," said Boris. "My hour has come."

Nobles returned to the council chamber. Boris rose and confronted them. "Ah, stop," he said. "I am still tsar." Then, "I die. God forgive me." He pointed to his son. "There! There is your tsar . . . . Have mercy—have mercy!" He fell, and the noblemen bowed their heads, murmuring, "He is dead."

Hänsel and Gretel

ENGELBERT HUMPERDINCK, *in 1891, was teaching and composing in Frankfort. His sister, Adelheid Wette, asked him to compose music to a few lines of verse. The song was to be sung in a children's play she was making of the Grimm fairy tale* Hänsel and Gretel.

Frau Wette was so delighted with the music her brother composed that she suggested the play be turned into an opera. Acting on her suggestion, Humperdinck composed Hänsel and Gretel, *which was first performed at Weimar on December 23, 1893.*

ACT I

HÄNSEL AND GRETEL, brother and sister, were alone in their poor home in the Harz Mountains of Germany. The cottage walls were hung with brooms—the children's father was a broommaker by trade—and Hänsel was making still another broom to add to the stock. Gretel sat knitting. She sang cheerfully at her work, but Hänsel could think only of how little they had to eat. "For weeks I've had nothing but bread," he said, and he tortured himself with thoughts of eggs and butter and suet paste.

Gretel tried to put him in a happier mood by singing to him, and she offered to tell him a secret if he would stop complaining. The secret was that a neighbor had given them some fresh milk. "It's here in the jug," she said, "and when mother comes home, she will surely make us a pudding."

Hänsel danced for joy. He tasted the cream on the milk, and Gretel rapped his fingers and ordered him back to his broom.

But Hänsel was weary of work. Dancing was much more fun, he said, and Gretel agreed. Making their own music by singing and clapping their hands, they danced together. They spun around and around until they lost their balance and tumbled to the floor.

The door opened. The children's mother came in. Embarrassed, Hänsel and Gretel got to their feet.

"What is all this?" asked their mother sharply.

"It was Hänsel—" began Gretel.

"It was Gretel—" interrupted Hänsel.

"Silence!" said their mother, and she scolded them for neglecting their work while their parents slaved from morning till night. She boxed Hänsel's ears, and with the sweep of her hand she upset the milk jug.

"Now what can I have for supper!" she said, weeping.

Hänsel laughed at the sight of her with milk streaming down her dress. She started toward him with a stick, and

he ran outside. "Wait till your father comes home!" she shouted. She snatched up a basket and thrust it into Gretel's hand. "Off to the wood!" she ordered the children. "Look for strawberries, and if you don't bring back the basket full, I'll whip you both!"

Hänsel and Gretel hurried off together. Their mother sank into a chair. "I have nothing to give them," she sobbed. "Not a crumb for my starving children."

She bowed her head on the table and wearily dropped off to sleep.

The broommaker entered with a basket on his back. He wakened his wife with a kiss. "What have we got to eat to-night?" he asked.

"Nothing," she answered, "and plenty of it."

He began to unpack his basket, while she looked on in amazement. He had brought enough food for a feast.

She lighted a fire and began to prepare supper, while he told her about his good fortune. There was a fair in town, and his brooms were in demand. He had sold them at the highest prices.

Suddenly he noticed that the children were not there. He asked where they had gone.

They were in the woods, his wife answered. The father was dismayed to think that their children were alone in the gloomy wood where the evil one lived.

The mother was alarmed. "What do you mean?" she asked.

A witch lived in the wood, he said—a wicked witch who rode on a broomstick and gobbled up boys and girls.

"Oh, horror!" cried the mother, and she and her husband ran out of the house in the direction the children had taken.

ACT II

Hänsel and Gretel were deep in the forest. She was sitting under a fir tree, making a wreath of wild roses. He was among the bushes, looking for strawberries.

Gretel sang quietly to herself, a song about a little man who stood silent and alone in the woods. Hänsel came out of the bushes. His basket was nearly filled with strawberries.

"Won't mother be pleased?" he said.

Gretel had finished her wreath. He put it on her head. "You shall be queen of the wood," he said, and ceremoniously presented her with the basket of strawberries.

A cuckoo called from among the trees. The children answered, imitating the cuckoo, who, they said, was a greedy bird and took what did not belong to it. In further imitation of the cuckoo, each ate a strawberry, then another. Soon they were quarreling over the berries, snatching them from each other until the basket was empty.

Gretel was shocked to realize that they had eaten the whole basket of strawberries. They must hurry and find more, she said.

But evening had come. In the darkness they could not see the berries.

"Oh, Hänsel, what shall we do?" cried Gretel. "We've been bad, disobedient children. We should have gone home sooner."

Again they heard the cuckoo, nearer than before. Hänsel looked about uneasily. All at once the forest was frightening, and the children did not know the way home.

A mist rose. Trees and bushes seemed to take on the forms of shadowy women who nodded and beckoned. Gretel was terrified, and she hid behind Hänsel.

"See there, sister," he said.

The mist had lifted a little, disclosing the Sandman, a small, gray figure with a sack on his back. He spoke gently to the children, threw some of his sand into their eyes, and disappeared.

The children were calm now, and half asleep.

"Sandman was there," said Hänsel drowsily. He and Gretel knelt and said their evening prayer, which began: "When at night I go to sleep, fourteen angels watch do keep." They lay down on a bed of moss and closed their eyes.

A soft light broke through the trees. A staircase appeared out of the mist. Down the stairs came fourteen angels, two by two, and placed themselves about the sleeping children.

ACT III

Morning had come. The angels were gone. The Dewman came and shook dewdrops on the children, and, when they began to stir, he stole away.

Gretel sat up and rubbed her eyes. She wakened Hänsel, who rose with a start. They told each other of the dreams they had had. Both had dreamed of fourteen angels gliding down a golden staircase.

They gazed about them. The mist had cleared away, and there before them stood a lovely little cottage. On one side was an oven. On the other was a stable joined to the house by a fence of gingerbread figures.

"Oh, magic castle, how good you would be to eat!" said the children, for the walls were made of pastry, the windows were of sugar, and the roof was of cake. It must be the house of a princess, they thought, and they were sure she would invite them in for a feast if only she knew how hungry and poor they were.

The cottage seemed to smile invitingly. They went near it. Hänsel broke a bit of cake from the roof.

A voice came from inside the house, "Nibble, nibble, mousekin, who's nibbling at my housekin?"

Hänsel dropped the piece of cake. The children stood listening, not sure they had really heard the voice.

Gretel picked up the cake. She and Hänsel tasted it, and they sighed in rapture. Hänsel broke another piece of cake off the roof.

From inside, the voice spoke again. The door opened, and a witch looked out. While the children were feasting, she stole up behind them and threw a rope about Hänsel's neck.

"Angels, you've come to visit me!" she said.

"Who are you, ugly one?" asked Hänsel. "Let me go."

The witch pretended great friendliness. She tried to coax them into the house with promises of delicious things to eat. All the time, Hänsel had been trying to free himself from the rope. He succeeded at last, and he and Gretel started to run away.

The witch held up the stick she carried. She spoke the words of a magic spell, and the children stopped. The head of the stick began to glow. Hänsel and Gretel stared at it, unable to turn their eyes away.

The witch led Hänsel into the stable and closed the lattice door after him. She said to Gretel, "I'll go inside to make things ready. You stay here where you are."

When the witch was gone, Hänsel spoke through the lattice to Gretel, "Watch well and see what she intends to do to me."

The witch returned and set before Hänsel a basket of almonds and raisins. "Now, little one, enjoy yourself," she said. She gestured with a juniper branch, releasing Gretel from her spell, and she sent the girl to set the table.

Gretel went away. The witch peered into the oven, and the red glow of the fire lighted her face. Gleefully she planned what she would do. First she would dine off Gretel as soon as the magic fire had baked the girl into gingerbread.

Shrieking and cackling in delighted anticipation, she rode about on a broomstick. She woke Hänsel and asked to see his thumb. He poked a small bone out through the lattice, and she exclaimed that he was much too thin.

"Gretel, bring raisins and almonds," she called. "Hänsel wants more to eat."

Gretel brought out a basket filled with raisins and almonds. The witch began to feed Hänsel. Gretel stepped behind her and gestured with the juniper branch. She spoke the magic words she had heard the witch use and secretly released her brother from the spell.

The witch opened the oven door. Hänsel made violent warning signs to Gretel.

"Come, my sugar-maiden," said the witch. "Peep into the oven and see if the gingerbread is ready."

Hänsel slipped out of the stable. "Sister, have a care," he whispered.

Gretel pretended to be awkward and dull-witted. She said to the witch, "I don't understand what I have to do."

"Just stand on tip-toe with your head bent forward," said the witch.

"Show me how to stand on tip-toe," said Gretel.

Impatiently the witch went to the oven and demonstrated what Gretel was to do. As she bent over, both the children rushed upon her and gave her a push. She tumbled into the oven, and they slammed the door.

The children fell into each other's arms. They sang and danced. Hänsel ran into the house and began to throw out fruit and nuts, which Gretel caught in her apron.

The fire was leaping high. The oven popped and crackled and fell in with a crash. Hänsel and Gretel stood amazed, as they saw themselves surrounded by a group of children —the gingerbread children whose covering of cake had fallen away.

"We are saved!" they shouted.

"Your eyes are shut—pray who are you?" asked Gretel.

"Touch us, that we may all awake," said the children.

Gretel caressed each child, and at her touch, each one opened his eyes and smiled. Still they were not able to move from the spot.

Hänsel took up the juniper branch, spoke the witch's incantation, and the children began to run and flock about him and Gretel.

"The spell is broken. We are free," they sang.

Hänsel and Gretel's father and mother appeared.

"Ho! They are here!" said their father, and the children joyfully ran to their parents.

Two of the other children had dragged the witch out of the magic oven. She was baked into a huge gingerbread cake, which the children set up in front of the house.

"See how the witch herself was caught," said the father, and the others repeated his words.

"This is heaven's punishment," he told them. He recited a verse for them to remember: "When past bearing is our grief, then 'tis heaven will send relief."

And again the others echoed his words.

Manon Lescaut

MANON LESCAUT *was Giacomo Puccini's third opera and his first great operatic success. The story was based on a novel by Abbé Prévost. In the matter of librettos Puccini was not easily pleased, and the final text was the work of five librettists.* Manon Lescaut *was first performed in Turin on February 1, 1893.*

ACT I

STUDENTS, townspeople, and soldiers had gathered in a square in Amiens. Edmondo, one of the students, dramatically hailed the coming night. His friends interrupted, laughing at his grand manner. Girls came down the avenue and past the inn, on their way home from work, and the men tried to attract their attention.

A young gentleman, the Chevalier Des Grieux, entered the square. He was dressed as a student. Edmondo spoke to him, but Des Grieux walked past without answering.

Edmondo concluded that his friend must be in love.

Love was either a tragedy or a farce, said Des Grieux. "I have no notion of it."

Edmondo and the other students insisted that Des Grieux was hiding some romantic adventure.

"No, but if you wish, I'll content you," said Des Grieux.

He spoke to some of the girls, pretending to be searching for his loved one among them.

The coach arrived from a neighboring village, and people pushed forward to see who had arrived. Among the passengers were Lescaut, a sergeant of the king's guards, Manon, his sister, and Geronte, an elderly gallant of Paris.

Lescaut signaled his sister to wait for him, and he and Geronte went into the inn.

Des Grieux spoke to the girl and asked her name.

"Manon Lescaut, they call me," she said.

Earnestly he told her that some spell had drawn him to her, and he asked how long she would be in Amiens.

"I leave at dawn," she answered sadly. "A convent awaits me."

This was a cruel fate for one so young and beautiful, he said. He asked if they could not meet again.

She heard her brother calling her. "I must go," she said, but before she left the square she promised to come back later that night.

He watched her out of sight. He had fallen suddenly and passionately in love, and he recalled the charming simplicity of her manner and the music of her voice. The students surrounded him noisily, warning him that his heart was in danger. Des Grieux was annoyed. He pushed them aside and went away.

Lescaut and Geronte came out of the inn. They had struck up an acquaintance on the coach, and now they were discreetly questioning each other. Geronte learned that Manon was soon to take the veil. Lescaut learned that Geronte was wealthy.

Some of the students were playing cards, and Lescaut made a place for himself at the table.

It was growing dark, and servants brought lamps and candles to light the front of the inn.

Geronte called the innkeeper and made an agreement with him. In an hour the innkeeper was to have a carriage and fast horses ready behind the inn. "A man will come there with a maiden, and they will gallop off to Paris," said Geronte. He paid the innkeeper in advance, and they left the square together.

Edmondo had drawn near and eavesdropped on the conversation.

Des Grieux entered. Edmondo told him that Geronte planned to carry Manon off to Paris. Des Grieux was startled and anxious. The two men plotted to thwart Geronte, and Edmondo called on his student friends for help.

Lescaut was drinking with the students. Unseen by him, Manon came out of the inn and went to Des Grieux. She had kept her word, she said, although she felt she should not have promised to meet him.

"Your words sound grave and alarming," he said, and he asked her not to look so sad.

"Once I was happy," she sighed. "Our home knew the sound of my laughter, and I often went dancing. But these days of pleasure soon ended."

Des Grieux declared his love for her. "Let love bring you happiness," he said.

She replied that she could see only sadness in her future.

In front of the inn Lescaut rose and called for more wine. The students shoved him back into his chair, deliberately keeping him there. The card game went on.

The sound of her brother's voice had frightened Manon. She turned back toward the inn. Des Grieux stopped her. "Listen," he said, and he told her of Geronte's plan to carry her away.

Edmondo came running up to them. "The carriage is ready," he said. "Oh, what a joke! Quick—be off!"

"What! Elope?" exclaimed Manon.

"With me, love," said Des Grieux.

For a few moments she resisted, then she yielded to the persuasion of Des Grieux and Edmondo. "I'll come," she said with decision. Manon and the two men hurried away.

Geronte came into the square, saw Lescaut engrossed in the card game, and looked pleased. "Now is the time," he said to himself. He called the innkeeper. "Is supper ready?" he asked.

"Yes, your excellency," said the innkeeper.

"Then announce it to that young lady—" began Geronte. Edmondo had returned. "That young lady?" he said. "There she goes. She's off with that young student," and he pointed down the road to Paris.

Geronte cried to Lescaut, "She is running away!"

"What!" shouted Lescaut.

"We must follow fast," said Geronte.

"Are any horses ready?" asked Lescaut.

Geronte shook his head, and Lescaut realized there was no hope of overtaking Manon and Des Grieux. He said, "I see that you have feelings of paternal affection for her."

"That is true," said Geronte.

"Then let me advise you as a devoted son," said Lescaut. "Go to Paris. The purse of a young student will soon be empty. Manon will be thankful to accept your help. You will act as a father to her, and I will complete the pleasant family party."

The students were laughing among themselves. Lescaut scowled at them fiercely, and offered his arm to Geronte.

ACT II

Manon was seated at her dressing table in Geronte's home in Paris. A hairdresser and two assistants were attending her. Lescaut entered. The hairdresser finished his work, and he and his assistants went away.

Lescaut looked admiringly at his sister. He was happy to have saved her from a life with the poor young student, he said. Des Grieux was a pleasant fellow, but he had no bal-

ance at the bank. "So it was right and proper," he concluded, "that Manon should leave that humble dwelling
for this gorgeous mansion."

Hesitantly she asked for word of Des Grieux.

"He, like Geronte, is my friend and comrade," said Lescaut. "He is forever asking where you are. I tell him I don't
know." Lescaut went on to say that Des Grieux had become
a gambler and in winning a fortune he hoped to find the
path that would lead to Manon.

For a little while she was sad, thinking of Des Grieux.
But as she turned to the mirror her thoughts changed, her
eyes began to sparkle, and she asked, "Does not this gown
suit me to perfection?"

A group of singers entered and sang a madrigal that
Geronte had composed for her. Some of Geronte's friends
arrived, along with a small orchestra. Geronte himself appeared, followed by a dancing master.

Manon confided to her brother, "All these things are
very pretty, but they bore me."

Lescaut saw danger in her boredom. "I'm off to Des
Grieux," he said to himself, "and like a master, I'll arrange
events," and he went quietly away.

The dancing master gave Manon a lesson in the art of
the minuet. Afterward she and Geronte danced together,
and he and his friends praised her grace and beauty.

Someone suggested a stroll on the boulevard. "Join us
there at your leisure," Geronte said to Manon, and he and
the others left her.

For a while longer she admired herself in the mirror. She
was preparing to leave, when Des Grieux came into the
room.

"You, my love!" she cried.

"Ah, Manon!" he said bitterly.

"You love me no more?" she said. "I admit I was to blame. I pray you to forgive me."

She knelt before him. He could not resist her charm. "I love you!" he said.

She rose and threw her arms about him.

Unexpectedly Geronte returned. The two men faced each other with open hostility. Manon placed herself between them.

Geronte said to her, "Is this your gratitude for the proofs of love I gave you?"

"What love, sir?" returned Manon. She held a mirror before his aging face, then pointed to the youthful Des Grieux.

Wounded and angry, Geronte bade them adieu. "We'll meet again, my pretty lady—and quickly," he said ominously, as he went away.

"Ah, we are free as the air!" Manon said to Des Grieux.

"We must leave here at once," he said, and she could not help feeling regret at the thought of giving up the luxury of Geronte's home.

He accused her of having been conquered by worldly pleasures. Yet he, too, had yielded, he confessed. He had become a gambler. "My shame and sorrow bring me back to you," he said despairingly.

"Forgive me once more," she said. "I shall be faithful— I swear it!"

Lescaut returned with frightening news. Geronte had ordered Manon's arrest.

"Go quickly!" he said, and Des Grieux urged her to make

haste, but Manon could not bear to leave all her treasures. She gathered up jewelry and hid it under her cloak.

From the balcony Lescaut saw police officers surrounding the house. When Manon ran to the door Geronte and the police were there before her. The jewelry she had taken began to fall from under her coat. The police officers seized her.

Des Grieux drew his sword. Lescaut took it from him. "If they arrest you," he said, "who will save Manon?"

The police dragged her away, and Des Grieux cried after her, "Oh, my Manon!"

ACT III

Des Grieux and Lescaut had come to Le Havre. In the hour before dawn they waited near the harbor where a ship was anchored.

The men were watching the sentinel who guarded the barracks. "Soon the guard I have bribed will take his turn," said Lescaut. Then they would be free to speak with Manon, who was a prisoner in the barracks. Geronte had had his revenge. Manon had been tried and sentenced to exile.

The guard was changed. At a sign from Lescaut, the new sentinel retired. A window of the barracks opened, and Manon looked out. She reached through the bars, and Des Grieux kissed her hands.

"She shall never leave!" said Lescaut, and he started off down the street.

Manon said to Des Grieux, "You do not forsake me?"

"Never. Soon you will be mine," he promised.

They were silent as a lamplighter walked past. Humming a tune, he put out the light on the street corner and went away.

Des Grieux told Manon to be ready. Lescaut had gone to bring help, and she would soon be free.

"I am afraid for you," she said. "I am afraid without knowing why."

Des Grieux started at the sound of a shot. Men began to shout, "To arms!" Lescaut came running up the street. The plot to rescue Manon had been discovered. "Save yourself!" he cried.

Manon begged Des Grieux to escape, and he fled with Lescaut.

Crowds poured into the square in front of the barracks. People were asking one another what had happened. A sergeant ordered them back.

The barracks gate opened. Soldiers came out, conducting a group of women in chains. The captain of the ship

came ashore with a company of sailors. The sergeant began a roll call of the prisoners. As each woman answered to her name, she walked toward the ship. The townspeople looked on, some with contempt, a few with sympathy.

Lescaut had returned and joined the onlookers. Des Grieux, too, was in the crowd. Manon walked past and saw him, and they clasped each other's hands.

Lescaut told the people about him, "See that young fellow? He is here to visit the girl who was stolen from him."

Manon bade Des Grieux farewell. The sergeant tried to push her toward the other women, but Des Grieux held her close to him. The crowd shouted encouragement to him and Manon.

"What's this?" asked the captain.

Des Grieux spoke with desperate courage, "While I live, no one shall take her from me!" He pleaded with the captain, "Hear me. Take me with you as a servant!"

The sergeant had separated Manon from Des Grieux and was driving the women toward the ship. The crowd watched, silent and compassionate.

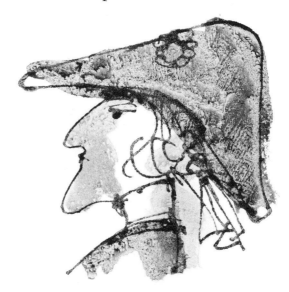

The captain was touched by Des Grieux' entreaty. "It shall be as you wish," he said. "Come, I'll take you."

Manon held out her arms, and Des Grieux rushed into them.

ACT IV

At nightfall Manon and Des Grieux were making their way across a plain in the French colony of Louisiana. They had walked a long distance. She was ill, and he supported her with difficulty.

"I must rest for a moment," she said faintly.

He left in search of water. Before long he returned, saying there was no water to be found.

She asked him to try to find shelter. He hesitated at leaving her alone again, then slowly he went away.

Fear and loneliness overwhelmed her. She had hoped for a peaceful life here. Now she was dying. "Do not let me die—help me!" she cried.

Des Grieux returned and came to her side. She tried to smile. She asked if he had brought good tidings, but he had found no shelter.

She sank to the ground. He touched her cheek and in her coldness he seemed to feel the chill of death.

"I cannot live without you!" he said. "I, too, shall die!"

"You shall not," she said in a solemn tone of command. She spoke her dying words, "Time will erase my faults, but my love will never die."

Overcome with grief, Des Grieux fell senseless beside her body.

Andrea Chénier

ANDREA CHÉNIER was composed by Umberto Giordano. The librettist, Luigi Illica, based his text on the life of André de Chénier, a poet of the French Revolution. At its first performance—in Milan, on March 28, 1896—the opera was a brilliant success.

ACT I

SERVANTS were preparing for a grand ball in the home of the Countess de Coigny near Paris. Directed by an arrogant major-domo, they hurried about the ballroom, carrying vases, flowers, and furniture. Gérard, a footman, helped carry a large blue sofa into the room.

"Put it down there," said the major-domo, and when the sofa was in place, he led the servants away.

Gérard remained behind. His father, also a servant of the house, came into the ballroom, staggering under the weight of a heavy flower-stand. Gérard went to help him.

After the old man had gone, his son reflected that his father's life had been wasted in devotion to thankless masters. He looked about the luxurious room, hating it as a symbol of the vain, empty world he despised.

Madeleine, the countess' daughter, entered with her maid, Bersi. Gérard watched the lovely Madeleine, whom he secretly adored.

The countess swept into the room, summoned the ser-

vants, and ordered them to light the candles. Madeleine
was not yet ready for the ball, and she sighed at the
thought of struggling into an uncomfortably fashionable
gown. She left quickly, as guests began to arrive. The
major-domo announced each one, and the countess greeted
them with flattering cordiality.

Several gentlemen were announced, including Fléville,
a novelist, and Andrea Chénier, a young poet. An abbé
arrived with the latest news from Paris. The king was weak
and ill-advised, he reported, and a mob had lately insulted
the statue of Henry the Fourth.

"Dreadful!" cried the guests, and the countess said pi-
ously, "They have no fear of God!"

Fléville proposed that they pass the evening happily, and
he introduced musicians and dancers, who came forward
and performed. The countess tried to persuade Chénier to
recite some of his poetry and was piqued when he refused.

Madeleine had returned. She wagered with some of her
friends that the poet would not refuse *her* request. She approached Chénier and asked him to favor them with
something of his own, something suitable for a nun or a
bride. Others drew near, expecting to be entertained.

Chénier disappointed them. The poem he recited was a
vigorous attack on the church and the ruling classes. There
was indignation among the guests, but Gérard, in the back
of the room, listened with burning sympathy.

Chénier begged Madeleine not to despise the words of a
poet.

She was strangely moved. "Please pardon me," she said,
ashamed of the frivolous wager she had made with her
friends.

The musicians were playing a gavotte. The countess called on the gentlemen to choose their partners. But as the dance was beginning, a dismal chant interrupted the music. Gérard opened the door and admitted a crowd of ragged peasants.

"His Highness, Prince Poverty!" he announced, mimicking the pompous manner of the major-domo.

"Who let them in here?" asked the countess angrily.

"It was I," said Gérard.

His father knelt before the countess in an attitude of supplication.

"Come," said Gérard. "She does not hear the voice of pity." He stripped off his livery and threw it at her feet. Footmen drove the peasants out. Gérard and his father went with them.

"That Gérard!" gasped the countess. "It is reading that

has ruined him. I've always been kind and generous—" She collapsed on the sofa, but quickly recovering, she asked the guests' pardon. "We'll finish the gavotte," she said, and once more the dance began.

ACT II

Several years had passed. The Revolution was raging. On a day in June, 1794, Andrea Chénier had come to the Café Hottot in Paris and was sitting alone at a sidewalk table. Mathieu, a Revolutionist, was nearby, dusting off a bust of the patriot, Marat. At another table sat Madeleine's maid, Bersi, talking with a man dressed as one of the Parisian dandies, who called themselves Incredibles. She was telling him of something she had heard—that Robespierre, leader of the Revolution, was sending spies among the people. "Is this true?" she asked.

"Not 'spies,'" said the man. "'Observers.' Why do you ask? Are you afraid?"

"I've nothing to fear," she answered. "Am I not a loyal daughter of the Revolution?"

A cart passed, carrying prisoners who had been sentenced to death.

Bersi finished her glass of wine and went away. The man, who was actually a spy, remembered that he had once seen her with a blonde-haired beauty. He had noticed, too, that Bersi had glanced slyly at Chénier, who seemed to be waiting for someone. "This bears watching," he said to himself, and he moved out of sight.

Roucher, a friend of Chénier, entered. The two men greeted each other.

"All day I've looked for you," said Roucher. "Here is your safeguard." He offered the poet a document.

"A passport?" said Chénier.

"You are in danger here," Roucher warned him. "Go, and save your life."

Chénier was unwilling to leave. He told his friend of the fascinating letters he had been receiving from an unknown woman. Some were playful, some serious. He had tried to guess who she might be, and at last he was to meet her. He was waiting for her now. He showed Roucher the letter in which she had promised to come to the café.

His friend advised him to throw away the letter and take the passport. The woman was probably someone quite unworthy, he said.

Gérard appeared in the street, leading a group of Revolutionists. Robespierre and other leaders of the Revolution passed by, while the cheering crowd shouted their names.

The spy had returned. Gérard joined him.

"The lady you ordered me to seek, is she pale and fair?" asked the spy.

Gérard answered that she was, and he described her in detail. "Find her, I beg you," he said. "Now that I have lost her, life is torture to me."

"This evening you shall see her," said the spy.

Gérard returned to his men and led them on down the street. The crowds moved away.

Bersi came by and whispered to Roucher, "Keep Chénier here. I'm being watched now."

The spy stepped in front of her and invited her into the café. They went inside together.

Chénier felt sure that the woman had nothing important

to tell him. He and Roucher were on the point of leaving, when Bersi came out of the café. She believed she had escaped the spy, but he was following close behind her. Hiding behind a jardiniere, he listened.

"Andrea Chénier," said Bersi, "in a little while a lady will come to you here. Wait for her."

"Tell me her name," said Chénier.

"Her name is—Hope," answered Bersi.

"Hope" was the name signed to the last letter from the unknown lady.

"I'll wait," said Chénier, and Bersi went swiftly away.

"This is a trap," said Roucher.

"I have my sword," Chénier told him.

Roucher went away to wait and keep watch.

Night had fallen. Mathieu entered and stayed only long enough to place a light on the altar in front of Marat's statue. The spy had hidden himself around the corner of the café.

A woman came cautiously toward Chénier and spoke his name.

"Who are you?" he asked.

She turned her face toward the light.

"Madeleine de Coigny!" he exclaimed.

The spy, too, had seen her face. He recognized her as the blonde woman sought by Gérard. "Now to tell him," he said, and he went quickly down the street.

Chénier reproached Madeleine for having kept herself so long unknown.

She answered that she had not dared to reveal herself. He had risen to power, while her life was in danger. When others of the nobility were being sent to the guillotine, she had been hidden and protected by her faithful friend, Bersi. But for a month she had been trailed by spies. Then came the news that Chénier had fallen from favor with the Revolutionists, and she had dared to come to him for help.

"You are my only hope," she said.

He declared his love for her, and promised himself to her in life and in death.

They started away together and came face to face with Gérard. "Madeleine de Coigny!" he said.

She stopped in horror.

Roucher and the spy entered at the same time. Chénier said to his friend, "Save her!" Gérard called out to the spy, "Follow her!"

Roucher held the spy off with pistols, and he and Madeleine escaped together. The spy ran for help.

Gérard and Chénier drew their swords and fought. Gérard fell, wounded. Looking up at his adversary, he recognized him for the first time as the poet he had long admired and respected.

"You are Chénier!" he said. "Your name is on the death
list . . . . Go! Save yourself and Madeleine."

Chénier fled.

The spy returned, bringing national guardsmen. Mathieu
entered and joined the crowd that had gathered about
Gérard.

"The man who attacked him is—" began the spy.

Gérard stopped him.

"The man who attacked him—?" asked the crowd.

"I do not know," said Gérard, and he fell back in a faint.

The enemies of the Revolution had committed this
crime, said Mathieu, and the crowd began to shout,
"Death! Death to them all!"

ACT III

In the court of the Revolutionary Tribunal Mathieu was
haranguing the people to give generously to freedom's
cause. A great urn had been set up in the center of the hall
to receive offerings, but few contributions had been made.
"Here comes Gérard," he said. "Maybe he can draw the
money from your pockets."

Gérard, almost recovered from his wound, addressed the
people in a rousing speech. Citizens crowded about the
urn, throwing in coins and trinkets.

A blind woman came forward, helped along by a boy of
fifteen. "I am old Madelon," she said. "My son is dead now.
He was killed at the seige of the Bastille. Here is his son,
the youngest, the last. Take him—for France."

"We will accept him," said Gérard, and the old woman
wept as she bade the boy good-by.

Gérard sat down at the table to prepare for the coming session of court. Mathieu swept the floor. The crowd moved outside and sang and danced in the street.

The spy entered with the news that Andrea Chénier had been captured, but Madeleine had not been found. "He has such an attraction for her that I think she will come back of her own accord," he said. He asked Gérard to draw up an indictment of Chénier.

Pen in hand, Gérard paused. "Why do I hesitate?" he asked himself. "Already his fate has been decided." Then he threw down his pen, saying vehemently, "No! It is vile!"

"Time is flying," said the spy.

Unwillingly Gérard wrote the indictment charging that Chénier was an enemy of his country. All the while he was saying to himself, "I thought myself a giant. I am still nothing more than a servant. I have only changed masters."

The spy read the charges and was satisfied. As he left the hall, the clerk of the tribunal came in. Gérard gave him a list of those who had been accused, and the clerk, too, left the courtroom.

Madeleine came before him. In a trembling voice she spoke. "Perhaps you no longer remember me. Ah, don't turn away. If you refuse to listen, I am lost!"

"I've been expecting you," said Gérard. "To bring you here, I've imprisoned your lover."

"Then take your revenge," she said.

He denied that he sought revenge. In the old days he had longed for her, he said, but he had been only a servant in her mother's home. Now their situations were changed. There was nothing to stand in the way of his great love. "Though you hate me, you will be mine," he said.

She turned to run out into the street. Then his meaning became clear to her. "If you will save his life," she said, "I am yours."

And Gérard said to himself, almost sobbing, "How she loves him!"

She told him of her life since the death of her mother. Her ancestral home had been burned. She had been ill and in constant danger. In those cruel times she had taken courage and found her only happiness in her love for Andrea Chénier.

Gérard was deeply moved by her story. He said in desperation, "He is lost. One who hates him has hurried his case before the tribunal."

She implored him to try to save Chénier.

Hastily he wrote a note to the president of the court. "Courage," he said. "I, his betrayer, will now defend him."

A noisy, excited crowd swarmed into the courtroom and settled down to watch the trial. The judge and jury took their places. Chénier was brought in with the other prisoners.

Fouquier-Tinville, the prosecutor, listened while the president read the names of the accused.

Chénier's name was read. He spoke in his own behalf, denying the charges of traitorous conduct. He was a soldier and a writer, he said. With his pen he had struck out at hypocrisy. With his poems he had glorified his country. "I am no traitor," he said. "Kill me if you will, but leave me my honor."

"The court will hear the witnesses," said Fouquier-Tinville.

Gérard faced the court. "The charge is false," he said.

Fouquier-Tinville was astonished. "Did you not write it?" he asked.

"But it is false," said Gérard.

"I deem the charges valid, and I reaffirm them," said the prosecutor.

"Here is your justice—an orgy of hate and vengeance!" cried Gérard. "Do not forget that we fought for freedom." He went to Chénier and embraced him. "Look—over there," he said softly.

Chénier saw Madeleine mingling with the crowd in the courtroom. "I've seen her once more," he said. "I die content."

"There is still hope," Gérard told him.

The jurors had gone out for their deliberation. Now they returned. The president read the verdict, "Death!" and Madeleine gave a despairing cry, "Andrea—Andrea!"

ACT IV

Chénier was writing by lantern light at a table in the courtyard of St. Lazare prison. Roucher had come to be with him.

Schmidt, a jailer, told Roucher, "Citizen, your time is up."

Roucher bribed the jailer so that he might stay a few minutes longer.

Chénier read the poem he had just written, his sad yet triumphant farewell to life.

The jailer came back, and the two friends parted. Schmidt opened the prison gate, admitting two more visitors—Gérard and Madeleine. Madeleine had been granted a final word with Chénier. She said to the jailer, "Among those who are to die tomorrow there is a young woman."

The woman's name was Legray, answered Schmidt.

"She must live," said Madeleine.

The man was puzzled as to how he could strike a name from the death roll.

"The name is nothing, if another woman takes her place," said Madeleine.

"But who will take her place?" asked Schmidt.

"I will," said Madeleine. "See here." She offered him gold and jewels.

"How can I refuse?" he said, accepting the bribe. "But remember, when the name Legray is called, step forward quickly."

"How to save them!" cried Gérard. "I'll go to Robespierre," and he rushed away.

Chénier came from the other side of the courtyard. He
greeted Madeleine with incredulous joy.

"There will be no farewell," she said. "I've come to die
with you. I go to death as Idia Legray."

In each other's arms they watched the daybreak. The
wheels of the death cart sounded on the stones.

The jailer began calling the prisoners' names: ". . . Andrea Chénier! . . . Idia Legray! . . ."

Chénier and Madeleine came forward together.

Louise

BOTH THE MUSIC and *libretto of* Louise *were written by Gustave Charpentier. The opera had its première performance in Paris on February 2, 1900, and was successful in spite of its controversial subject matter.* Louise *was one of the first French operas dealing with contemporary working people rather than nobility or legendary characters.*

ACT I

AT THE TURN of the century Louise, a young seamstress, lived with her mother and father in Paris. Her home was on the top floor of a lodginghouse. In the building opposite was the studio of Julien, an artist.

On an April evening Louise was at her balcony window, Julien was on the terrace outside his studio, and they were talking across the space between. They were in love and hoped to marry, but her parents opposed the match. "I love them so much. I love you so much," she said. "What can I do?"

While they reminisced about their few stolen meetings, Louise's mother came quietly up behind her daughter. She listened for a while, her indignation rising. Then she caught hold of Louise and dragged her out into the kitchen.

Julien said anxiously, "You don't talk any more. Answer me before your jailer comes back."

Louise's mother went to the window and said in a threatening voice, "Are you going to stop talking, or shall I come over and pull your ears!"

After a moment of astonishment, Julien began to laugh. Louise came out of the kitchen, and her mother separated the lovers by slamming the window shut.

Trembling, the girl took the provisions her mother had brought home and arranged them on the buffet. Angrily and mockingly her mother repeated part of the conversation she had overheard. "Oh, if your father knew of your goings-on, he would die!" she said.

"Why don't you let us marry?" pleaded the girl. "Why do you make me pretend? What objection can you have to him?"

"A rascal, a ne'er-do-well, a drunkard!" said her mother.

"If you think you can change me, you're mistaken," said Louise. "You may keep me from being happy, but you can't destroy our love."

Her father came home from work. His wife busied herself in the kitchen, Louise set the table, and he sat down to read the letter he had just received. Knowing the letter was from Julien, Louise looked away, embarrassed.

He watched her for a while. He held out his arms, and they embraced. Then Louise's mother brought in the soup, and the three sat down to their evening meal.

"What a day!" said Louise's father. "I am no longer young, and the days are long." Yet he must keep working, he said. If he quit, who would keep the pot boiling?

"And when one thinks of those who spend their lives enjoying themselves—" said his wife, glancing toward Julien's window.

"Everyone to his own fate," he answered. "We are happy as we are." In a playful mood, he lifted his wife out of her chair and tried to dance with her. "Stop! Let me go," she said crossly, freeing herself.

After the meal the family discussed Julien's letter. Once more the young man had asked for Louise's hand.

Louise's mother was indignant.

"Don't make a tragedy of it," said Louise's father. "We can easily inquire about him and find out if he is more set-tled now. We don't have to give Louise to him tomorrow, and he isn't going to carry her off. After I've talked with him—"

"If he comes here, I leave," declared Louise's mother. "That Bohemian, that barroom fixture. And I know a few other things about him—"

"It's not true!" Louise broke in, and her mother slapped her face.

Louise threw herself into a chair and wept, her father went to comfort her, and her mother sulkily retired into the kitchen and began to do the ironing.

"My child," said Louise's father, "at your age everything is rose-colored, and taking a husband is like choosing a doll. But there are all sorts of dolls, and some cause you to shed many tears."

"When one is good and gentle and loving—" began Louise.

"How would you choose?" he asked.

"With my heart," she said.

It was the poorest way to judge, he told her, because love was always blind. He asked if the young man had ever spoken to her of love.

Unwilling to tell her father the truth, she answered, "No." In the kitchen her mother was singing softly, weaving some of Julien's tender speeches into her song.

Louise's father looked at his daughter a little mistrustfully. He said, "If I refuse his request, will you promise to forget him? Will you promise to obey us as a daughter should? If you should ever turn away from me, I couldn't go on long."

She assured him she would always love him.

"Some day you'll thank me for saving you from pain and trouble. Here, read me the paper," he said cheerfully. "It will help you forget and save my poor eyes."

Louise's mother came in and sat down at the table with her mending. The girl read, " 'The spring season is most brilliant. All Paris is very gay . . .' Paris!" she repeated, and she began to sob.

ACT II

It was early morning, and already Montmartre had come alive. A milk woman was setting up her booth on the sidewalk. A paper girl was folding her newspapers. A ragman was at work, with a coal-gatherer and a scavenger busy nearby. Housekeepers passed on their way to market. Mingling with the people was the noctambulist—a nightwalker, on his way home after a round of pleasure.

From every side came shouts and street calls and fragments of conversation—the voice of Paris.

Julien appeared with a group of friends. He pointed out the doorway of the dressmaking shop where Louise worked. "Her mother will bring her here," he said. "I'll run and catch up with Louise, and if her parents have refused me again—"

"You'll carry her off," finished one of his friends, and the others shouted, "Bravo!"

Servant girls leaned out of windows, singing to the men and throwing them kisses.

Julien was feverish with impatience to see Louise again. "Now is the time," he said. "Leave me," and his friends wished him good luck and went away.

Street vendors cried their wares. Girls hurried past on their way to work. As Louise and her mother came down the street, Julien moved into hiding in a shed.

Louise's mother said sharply to her daughter, "What are you looking around for? I suppose he's following us. I'll ask your father to let you work at home after this."

Louise went into the shop. Her mother looked sus-

piciously about her before leaving. The moment she was gone, Julien dashed into the building and came out, pulling Louise along by the arm.

She said wildly, "Let me go!"

"Have they refused me?" he demanded. "Are you going to stand for that?"

She answered that her parents were the masters—she could do nothing.

"Have they the right to keep you a prisoner?" he asked.

"I'm going to be late," she said. "Let me go."

He declared that she no longer loved him. "If you loved me, would you forget your promise?" he said. Over and over he begged her to come away with him.

"I don't know what to do," she said. "Let me go. Tomorrow—later—"

She ran into the shop.

In the sewing room the seamstresses were sitting at tables, talking as they worked. Louise sat apart from the others. They noticed her silence and wondered why she looked so sad.

"I think she is in love," said one girl, and others took up her words. They talked of their sweethearts, and while the forewoman was out of the room, a girl began to sing, "A mysterious voice amid the sounds of the street pursues and captures me. It is the voice of Paris, the call to love and pleasure . . ."

Trumpets sounded outside. Seamstresses went to the window. A small orchestra had gathered below, prepared to accompany a singer. The singer was Julien.

"He seems to be singing to somebody here," said one of

the girls, and for a while they were charmed. But as the serenade went on, they wearied of it and began to laugh and jeer at the musicians.

Louise could bear no more. She took her hat from the rack and went to the door. "Tell Madam I had to go," she said.

"She is ill," said one seamstress.

"It's the singer's fault," said another.

From the window they saw Louise outside in the street. They watched in amazement. Louise and the singer were hurrying off together!

ACT III

At dusk, in the garden of their home in Montmartre, Louise and Julien looked out over Paris. Ever since they had been together, she told him, she had been almost incredibly happy.

"You have no regrets?" he asked.

"None," she said. "At the shop I was a stranger. At home my father treated me as if I were a child. And from my mother, nothing but rebuffs and blows."

"Mother Routine and Father Prejudice," said Julien. "They understand each other well."

They walked across the garden and gazed on the panorama before them. "The music of the great city!" she said.

"The city has given you to me," he said, and she answered, "My love will give you the city."

Night was coming on. The lights of Paris began to glimmer, and the city seemed to be calling to Louise and Julien, "You are free!"

They went into their house. People of Montmartre began to descend on the little garden, carrying flags, draperies, and lanterns. They set to work decorating the doorway of the house. Fathers and mothers appeared, making critical remarks about the young people.

Julien and Louise came to the doorway. Their young Bohemian friends gathered about them. In a ceremony conducted by a man dressed as the Father of Fools, Louise was crowned Queen of Bohemia and Muse of Montmartre.

The young people admired her beauty. The mothers were outraged at her boldness, and the fathers watched the proceedings with contempt.

Caught up in the carnival spirit, Louise and Julien told each other joyously, "Nothing shall ever separate us!"

A hush fell. A woman had come up the steps leading to the garden. Some of the people recognized her. "Louise's mother," they said.

She came toward the house slowly and timidly, as if dazzled by the lights. Her face was drawn with misery. The crowd separated and disappeared.

Louise took refuge in the entrance of the house. Julien guarded the door as if from an enemy.

But Louise's mother spoke humbly. "I came to say to Louise that her father is suffering and only she can save him."

"My father!" whispered Louise.

Her mother said to Julien, "Today he is much worse. Please let her come back home."

"Is he very sick?" asked Louise.

Her mother told her how he had wept, how he had
walked the floor at night. Now he was ill. "Only a great
joy can save him," she said, appealing to Julien. "You can
give it to him by letting Louise come home. She will be
free. What we want is to have her only for a little while."

The old ragman passed by, singing of his daughter whom
he had lost forever in the maze of the great city. Julien was
touched by the song. He asked Louise's mother, "Do you
promise to give her back to me?"

"I promise," she said.

"Then go," he said to Louise, "and remember that from
this time on, I'll count every hour."

She bade him a tearful farewell and followed her mother
out of the garden.

ACT IV

On a summer evening Louise's father was at home.
Seated at the table, he covertly gazed through the doorway of Louise's room where the girl sat sewing.

Louise's mother brought him a cup of tea, then went to
open the window. The building where Julien had once
lived had been torn down, and in the opening was a view
of Paris.

"You ought to go to the window," she said. "We can
breathe now. See the big tunnel of air and light and life."

Louise's father continued to sit at the table, looking
wretched and gloomy.

"Maybe you shouldn't have worked so hard today," she
said.

He answered that his illness was gone and he was perfectly well. Still watching his daughter, he lamented the
ingratitude of children, and he cursed the man who had
made Louise a stranger to her parents.

Louise's mother went into the kitchen and called the
girl, "Come and help me."

Louise came out of her room. She walked past her father
without looking at him and went into the kitchen.

"Will you stop sulking?" her mother scolded her. "Maybe
you think we are going to let you go back to that man."

"You promised it," said Louise.

"You must know it's impossible," said her mother. "We
can't let you go back to such a life." She ordered Louise to
bed. "And don't forget to say good night to your father."

Louise said good night to him. He held her in a long
embrace. She moved coldly away from him. He caught her
in his arms again and forced her to sit on his knee. "Why
do you want to go?" he said. "Is there a safer place on
earth than your father's heart?"

She asked if he imagined she could be happy living like
a captive.

"If you want to be free, give up your dream of folly," he
said.

"You wish me to be false to my promises as you were
false in yours," she said.

"The liberty you ask for is freedom to dishonor yourself," he said. He seated her on his knee again and tried to
tell her how much he loved her.

She tore herself away from him. "All beings have the
right to be free," she declared. "Every heart has the right
to love."

"You speak as a stranger, an enemy," he said, "not as my daughter, my hope, my pretty one."

Distant voices seemed to repeat the words, "Pretty one!" To Louise the echo was the voice of Paris, calling her.

"Oh, the magic!" she exclaimed in sudden delight. "The dear music of the city!"

He slammed the window, shutting out the alluring sights and sounds.

But a kind of madness had seized the girl. She flung herself about the room, crying out that she was waiting for her beloved to come and carry her away.

In shocked voices her father and mother ordered her to be quiet.

"I am not a fearful little girl any longer," she said defiantly, and she ran to the door. Her father blocked her way.

"Julien, come to me, Julien!" she called.

Shaking with fury, her father stepped aside. "You miserable creature, go and find him!" he shouted. "Will you get out, or shall I throw you through the door?"

He reached for her. His wife tried to hold him back. He pushed her aside and she fell. Louise ran past him and out through the doorway.

Almost at once his anger was gone. He stumbled out into the hallway. In a pleading voice he called down the stairs, "Louise—Louise!"

His wife went to the window and looked out into the night. He came back into the room and stood listening to the street sounds. He spoke, shaking his fist with hatred at the enemy that had taken his daughter from him, "Oh, Paris!"

Pelléas and Mélisande

PELLÉAS AND MÉLISANDE *is Claude Debussy's only opera. It was begun in 1892 and finished ten years later. The libretto is from a play by Maeterlinck. The opera had its first performance in Paris on April 30, 1902, and public reaction was sharply divided.* Pelléas and Mélisande *was a new and revolutionary kind of music drama, subtle and dreamlike, with little action and few climaxes. The work is still controversial, but over the years it has gained a place among the world's operatic masterpieces.*

ACT I

A HUNTER, lost in the forest, came upon a frail, childlike girl weeping beside a fountain. She rose in fright when he touched her shoulder.

"Do not touch me," she said, "or I shall throw myself into the water!"

He meant her no harm, he said, and he asked, "Has anyone hurt you?"

"Oh, yes, yes, yes!" she said, but she would not say what harm had come to her. Neither would she tell him where she had come from. "I escaped," she said, "I am lost."

He saw something sparkling in the water.

"It is the crown he gave me," she said, but she would not tell who had given it to her, and when he offered to recover it, she answered that she no longer wanted it.

"Who are you?" she asked.

He replied that he was Prince Golaud, grandson of King Arkel, who ruled the country.

"Why did you come here?" she asked.

"I was hunting in the forest. I followed a boar," he said. He asked her to go with him. She refused.

"You cannot stay here all night— What is your name?" he asked.

"Mélisande," she told him.

"You cannot stay here, Mélisande," he said. "Come, give me your hand."

She asked where he was going.

"I do not know," he said. "I am lost, too."

King Arkel and his daughter-in-law, Geneviève, were together in the castle. The king was almost blind, and Geneviève was reading him a message from her son, Golaud—a letter Golaud had written to his young half-brother, Pelléas.

In the letter he told how he had found Mélisande. For six months they had been married, and still her past was a mystery to him. He feared the marriage would displease Arkel, since the king had wished him to marry someone else. "If, nevertheless, he consents to receive her," Golaud had written, "on the third evening following this letter, light a lamp in the tower that looks on the sea. I shall see it from our ship; if not, I shall sail on and never return."

Geneviève asked the king, "What do you say of it?"

"I say nothing of it," he answered calmly. "Let it be as he wishes."

"He has always been so prudent," said Geneviève. "Since the death of his wife, he lived only for Yniold, their little son." Now, she said, he had forgotten everything.

Pelléas entered. He had been weeping, and he told the king, "Grandfather, I have received a letter from my friend, Marcellus. He is about to die, and he calls me. If I am to arrive before his death, there is no time to lose."

"Wait a while," said Arkel. "We do not know what the return of your brother has in store for us." Besides, he added, Pelléas' father, ill in another part of the castle, was perhaps sicker than Pelléas' friend.

The king went away, and Geneviève told her son to light the lamp in the tower.

Golaud had returned with his bride, and Geneviève and Mélisande were walking about the castle grounds. They saw Pelléas coming toward them.

His mother called his name. He joined them. The three stood together and watched a ship leaving port. Mélisande recognized it as the ship that had brought her here.

Night was coming on. "It is time to go inside," said Geneviève. "Pelléas, show Mélisande the way. I must go to see the little Yniold for a moment."

She left them. Pelléas and Mélisande looked out on the sea and the beacon lights. The sound of the waves grew louder. A storm was breaking.

"Let us go this way," he said. "Give me your hand."

She showed him that her hands were full of flowers.

"I will support you by your arm. The way is steep and

dark," he said. He told her, "Tomorrow I go away, per-haps."

"Why do you go away?" she asked.

ACT II

Pelléas had led Mélisande to a spring near the castle. According to legend, its water could restore sight to the blind, he told her.

"If something sparkled at the bottom, one might be able to see it," she said, leaning over the pool and trying to touch the water.

He warned her to take care, and she drew back. "I cannot reach it," she said.

Pelléas recalled that it was on the edge of a fountain that Golaud had found her. "What did he say to you?" he asked.

She answered that she could no longer remember. Looking into the water, she played with the ring Golaud had given her.

"Do not throw it so high," he said. As he spoke, she dropped the ring and it fell into the pool.

"It is lost," she said. "What shall we do?"

He tried to reassure her. There was no need to be anxous over a ring, he told her.

"What shall we say to Golaud if he asks where it is?" she asked.

"The truth," he said.

*

That night Golaud lay in his bed in the castle. Mélisande sat near him. He was telling her he could not explain what had happened to him in the forest that day. "I was hunting quietly," he said. "I had just heard the stroke of noon. At the twelfth stroke my horse became frightened and ran into a tree. I fell, and he must have fallen on me."

It was on the stroke of noon that Mélisande had dropped the ring into the pool.

"Try to sleep," she said. "I will stay here all night."

"I will not let you tire yourself," he said.

Mélisande was weeping. She was not happy, she said, although she insisted that no one had offended her.

He asked if she wished to leave him.

"Oh, no. I would like to go away with you," she said, "but I feel I cannot live here any longer."

"Is it Pelléas?" he asked. "I think he does not often speak to you."

"He speaks to me," she said. "I think he does not like me, but he speaks when we meet."

Golaud tried to guess what was wrong. Perhaps the life they led was too sad. Perhaps the castle was too old and cold and somber and the days were too dark.

It was true, she said, one never saw the clear sky.

"So that is why you weep. Come, you are no longer a child, to weep at such things," he said. Trying to console her, he took her hands in his. He saw that the ring was gone.

"Our wedding ring, where is it?" he asked.

She said in confusion, "I think it fell . . ." She pretended she had lost it in a grotto on the seashore where she had gone to gather shells for little Yniold.

He ordered her to go and look for it.

"Now, in the dark?" she asked.

"Now, at once," he said. "I would sooner lose all I have than to lose this ring. You do not know what it is. Hurry, before the sea comes and takes it."

"I dare not go alone," she said.

"Ask Pelléas to go with you," he said.

On the shore Pelléas and Mélisande waited for the moon

to shine and light their way. He had brought her here so that she could describe the grotto to Golaud, to convince him that she had really come in search of the ring.

Moonlight broke through the clouds, lighting the opening of the grotto. A little way inside, three old white-haired men were sleeping, and Pelléas believed this to be a sign of famine in the land.

Mélisande said fearfully, "Let us go!"

"Take care, do not awaken them," he said. "Come."

"Let me be," she said. "I prefer to walk alone."

"We will return another day," he said, and they left the grotto.

ACT III

By starlight Mélisande sat at a tower window in the castle. She sang as she combed her hair. Pelléas came along the path below and asked her to lean forward so that he could see her loosened hair. When she leaned out the window he exclaimed, "How beautiful you are! Give me your hand tonight before I go away. I leave tomorrow."

"No, no, no," she said, and she quickly persuaded him not to go. She extended her hand to him. Her long hair fell about his face. He caught it in his arms, holding it close to him.

"Let me go," she cried. "You will make me fall!"

He tied her hair to the branches of a willow so that she could not escape.

Two doves flew out of the tower and circled about them.

They were her doves, said Mélisande. She feared they would be lost and never come back. "Let me lift my head," she said. "I hear footsteps. I think it is Golaud."

But her hair was fastened in the willow branches, and Pelléas was slow in releasing her.

Golaud appeared. "What are you doing here?" he asked.

Pelléas was confused. "What am I doing?" he began. "I—"

"You are two children. Mélisande, do not lean from the window. You will fall. Do you not know it is late?" said Golaud, laughing nervously. "What children!"

He and Pelléas went away together.

The next morning Golaud led his brother into the dim vaults of the castle. Golaud told him, "Here is the stagnant water . . . Do you smell the odor of death that rises? Lean over. Do not be afraid. I will hold your arm. Do you see the abyss?"

Pelléas looked into the abyss. "I suffocate here," he said. "Let us go out."

"Yes, let us go out," said Golaud.

In silence they left the vaults.

Outside in the fresh air Pelléas breathed deeply. He heard the noon bells ring, and he saw Geneviève and Mélisande at a window in the tower.

Golaud spoke to him about Mélisande. "I heard what happened last night," he said. "I know those are children's games, but they must not be repeated. She may soon be a mother, and we must be very careful of her."

*

At night Golaud and his young son, Yniold, sat under Mélisande's window. Golaud questioned the boy. Were Mélisande and Pelléas often together? Was it true that they quarreled?

Yes, they were often together, answered the boy, and it was true that they quarreled. They quarreled about the door.

"About the door? Why?" asked Golaud.

"Because it cannot be opened," said Yniold.

"Tell me what you know about it!" demanded Golaud, but the boy, frightened by his father's intensity, began to weep and could tell no more about the door.

"I am not angry," said Golaud. "What do they talk about when they are together?"

"Of me," said Yniold. "They say I will become as big as you."

Golaud asked if they ever embraced each other.

"No, no," said his son. Then, recollecting, "Ah, yes; once—"

A light appeared in Mélisande's window. Golaud lifted the child, asking him to look in and tell him who was in the room.

Mélisande was there, said the child, and Pelléas, too. They were not speaking or moving, only looking at the light. "They never close their eyes," said Yniold. "I am afraid."

"Of what are you afraid?" asked Golaud.

"Let me down," begged the child. "I am going to cry out!"

Golaud let him down and took him away.

ACT IV

King Arkel had been ill, but now he was better. He had recognized Pelléas and said to him, "You have the grave and friendly face of one who will not live long. You must travel . . ."

Pelléas told this to Mélisande as they met in a passageway outside the king's room. They agreed to meet later near the fountain in the park. "It will be my last evening," he said. "I am about to travel. You will not see me again."

She did not believe him. "I will see you always," she said.

They separated and left the passageway. In a little while Mélisande returned with King Arkel. He had pitied her, he was saying, since her coming to this joyless house. She was too young and beautiful for such a life, and he predicted that her youth and beauty would open the door to a new happiness.

Golaud entered. "Pelléas goes away tonight," he said.

"You have blood on your forehead," said Arkel.

It was nothing, answered Golaud; he had passed through a thorny hedge.

Mélisande tried to wipe his forehead. He pushed her away. "Where is my sword?" he asked. "Why do you tremble? I am not going to kill you!"

He had grown distraught and violent. Holding her by the hair, he forced her to her knees.

"Golaud!" cried Arkel.

"You will do as you like," Golaud said, with a sudden, unnatural calm. "I do not attach any importance to it."

He went out.

"What ails him?" asked Arkel.

"He no longer loves me," she said.

"If I were God," said Arkel, "I would have pity for the hearts of men."

Beyond the castle Yniold was trying to lift a heavy stone. "It is heavier than all the world," he was saying. "I see my golden ball between these stones, and I cannot reach it."

He heard sheep bleating in the distance. He paused, watching them, watching the shepherd who drove them.

"It is not the way to the stable," said the child, with pity and fear in his heart. "Where will they sleep tonight?"

At the fountain in the park Pelléas waited for Mélisande. "It is the last evening," he said. "I must look at her one more time and tell her all I have not told her."

Mélisande appeared. He said again that he was going away. "You do not know why I must go. You do not know it is because I love you."

She answered, "I love you, too."

He was wildly excited. "You love me? Since when do you love me?"

"Since always," she said.

"Oh, how you say that!" he cried. "You do not lie a little to make me smile?"

"No, I lie only to your brother," she said.

They stood in the shadow of a tree. "We cannot see how happy we are," he said, and he asked her to come out into the moonlight.

"I am nearer to you in the darkness," she said.

While they stood there they heard the castle gate being closed for the night.

"We can no longer get in!" he said.

"All the better," she answered. There was a sound in the darkness. "Someone is behind us," she said. They saw Golaud standing motionless in the shadows.

"He does not know we have seen him," said Pelléas. "Go away. I will wait—I will stop him."

"No!" she said.

"He will kill us," said Pelléas.

"All the better," she said.

Sword in hand, Golaud threw himself upon them and struck Pelléas down. Mélisande fled into the wood. Golaud ran after her.

ACT V

At sunset Arkel, Golaud, and a physician had come to Mélisande's room. Mélisande lay in bed. Golaud was grief-stricken because he had killed his brother and wounded Mélisande, so that she might die. The physician said consolingly, "She could not die from this little wound."

"I killed without reason," said Golaud. "They were brother and sister, and I—"

The physician interrupted. "I think she awakens."

"Open the window," said Mélisande faintly.

Arkel opened it. He was happy to hear her speak clearly again. For the past several days she had been delirious. "If you are afraid of Golaud, he will go away," said the king.

"Golaud is here?" she said. "Why does he not come near me?"

Golaud went to the bed.

"I hardly recognized you with the evening sun in my eyes," she said. "You have grown thin and older."

Golaud wished to speak to her alone. He sent the others away. "Do you forgive me?" he asked.

"Yes, yes," she said.

"I have done you so much harm," he said miserably. "All that happened is my fault, but I loved you so much. It is I who will die, and I want to ask you— The truth must be told to one about to die. Do you swear to tell the truth?"

"Yes," she said.

"Did you love Pelléas?" he asked.

"Why, yes," she answered. "Where is he?"

"You do not understand," said Golaud. "I ask if you loved him with a forbidden love."

"No," she said. "Why do you ask that?"

"Do not lie any more, at the moment of dying!" he said in agony.

"Who is going to die?" she asked.

"You, and I after you—and we must have the truth!" he said.

"The truth—the truth—" she said vaguely.

Arkel and the physician returned. The king asked Mélisande if she wished to see her child.

"What child?" she said.

"Your little girl," he said.

"I cannot raise my arms to take her," said Mélisande.

Arkel lifted the child from the bed.

"She does not laugh. . . . She will always weep. I pity her," said Mélisande.

Maidservants of the castle began to enter the room. Silently they ranged themselves along the walls and stood as if waiting.

"Who called them?" asked Arkel, and Golaud said, "Why do you come here? Nobody asked you," but the servants did not answer.

Mélisande had closed her eyes. Golaud begged to be left alone with her again.

"Do not speak to her any more," said Arkel. "You do not know what the soul is."

The servants knelt. The physician went to the bed and found that Mélisande was dead.

Golaud was sobbing. Arkel said to him, "It is terrible, but it is not your fault. Come, it will not do for the child to stay in the room. It must live now in her place. It is the turn of the poor little one. . . ."

CASTS OF CHARACTERS

COSÌ FAN TUTTE
by Wolfgang Amadeus Mozart

Fiordiligi . . . . *Soprano*
Dorabella . . . . *Soprano*
Ferrando . . . . *Tenor*
Guglielmo . . . . *Baritone*
Don Alfonso . . . . *Bass-baritone*
Despina . . . . *Soprano*

FIDELIO
by Ludwig van Beethoven

Leonore . . . . *Soprano*
Florestan . . . . *Tenor*
Rocco . . . . *Bass*
Marzelline . . . . *Soprano*
Jaquino . . . . *Tenor*
Don Pizarro . . . . *Bass*
Don Fernando . . . . *Bass*

DER FREISCHÜTZ
by Carl Maria von Weber

Max . . . . *Tenor*
Kilian . . . . *Tenor*
Cuno . . . . *Bass*
Caspar . . . . *Bass*
Agathe . . . . *Soprano*
Aennchen . . . . *Soprano*
Hermit . . . . *Bass*
Prince Ottokar . . . . *Baritone*
Samiel . . . . *Spoken*

NORMA

by Vincenzo Bellini

Norma . . . . *Soprano*
Pollione . . . . *Tenor*
Flavio . . . . *Tenor*
Adalgisa . . . . *Mezzo-soprano*
Oroveso . . . . *Bass*
Clotilde . . . . *Soprano*

THE FLYING DUTCHMAN

by Richard Wagner

Daland . . . . *Bass*
The Dutchman . . . . *Baritone*
Senta . . . . *Soprano*
Erik . . . . *Tenor*
Mary . . . . *Contralto*
Steersman . . . . *Tenor*

SIMON BOCCANEGRA

by Giuseppe Verdi

Simon Boccanegra . . . . *Baritone*
Paolo . . . . *Bass*
Pietro . . . . *Bass*
Fiesco . . . . *Bass*
Amelia . . . . *Soprano*
Gabriele . . . . *Tenor*
Captain . . . . *Tenor*

UN BALLO IN MASCHERA

by Giuseppe Verdi

Richard . . . . *Tenor*
Renato . . . . *Baritone*
Amelia . . . . *Soprano*
Samuel . . . . *Bass*
Thomas . . . . *Bass*
Oscar . . . . *Soprano*
Ulrica . . . . *Contralto*
Sylvan . . . . *Baritone*

LA FORZA DEL DESTINO

by Giuseppe Verdi

Leonora . . . . *Soprano*
Marquis of Calatrava . . . . *Bass*
Curra . . . . *Mezzo-soprano*
Don Alvaro . . . . *Tenor*
Don Carlo . . . . *Baritone*
Preziosilla . . . . *Mezzo-soprano*
Melitone . . . . *Baritone*
Guardiano . . . . *Bass*
Alcalde . . . . *Bass*
Trabuco . . . . *Tenor*

DON CARLOS

by Giuseppe Verdi

Elizabeth . . . . *Soprano*
Don Carlos . . . . *Tenor*
Thibault . . . . *Soprano*
Lerma . . . . *Tenor*
Eboli . . . . *Mezzo-soprano*
Countess d'Aremberg . . . . *Mute*
Rodrigo . . . . *Baritone*
Philip . . . . *Bass*
Grand Inquisitor . . . . *Bass*
Friar . . . . *Bass*

OTELLO

by Giuseppe Verdi

Otello . . . . *Tenor*
Iago . . . . *Baritone*
Desdemona . . . . *Soprano*
Roderigo . . . . *Tenor*
Cassio . . . . *Tenor*
Montano . . . . *Bass*
Emilia . . . . *Mezzo-soprano*
Lodovico . . . . *Bass*

FALSTAFF

by Giuseppe Verdi

Falstaff	*Baritone*
Doctor Caius	*Tenor*
Bardolph	*Tenor*
Pistol	*Bass*
Alice Ford	*Soprano*
Anne Ford	*Soprano*
Meg Page	*Mezzo-soprano*
Dame Quickly	*Mezzo-soprano*
Ford	*Baritone*
Fenton	*Tenor*

THE BARTERED BRIDE

by Bedrich Smetana

Marie	*Soprano*
Hans	*Tenor*
Kezal	*Bass*
Kruschina	*Baritone*
Kathinka	*Soprano*
Wenzel	*Tenor*
Micha	*Bass*
Agnes	*Mezzo-soprano*
Springer	*Tenor*
Muff, East Indian	*Tenor*
Esmeralda	*Soprano*

LA GIOCONDA

by Amilcare Ponchielli

Gioconda	*Soprano*
Cieca	*Contralto*
Barnaba	*Baritone*
Alvise	*Bass*
Laura	*Mezzo-soprano*
Enzo	*Tenor*
Zuàne	*Bass*
Isèpo	*Tenor*

LAKMÉ

by Léo Delibes

Lakmé	*Soprano*
Nilakantha	*Bass-baritone*
Mallika	*Mezzo-soprano*
Hadji	*Tenor*
Ellen	*Soprano*
Rose	*Soprano*
Mrs. Benson	*Mezzo-soprano*
Gerald	*Tenor*
Frederic	*Baritone*

THE TALES OF HOFFMANN

by Jacques Offenbach

Hoffmann	Tenor
Lindorf	Bass
Andrès	Tenor
Nathanael	Tenor
Hermann	Baritone
Luther	Baritone
Nicklausse	Mezzo-soprano
Spalanzani	Tenor
Cochenille	Tenor
Coppélius	Baritone
Olympia	Soprano
Giulietta	Soprano
Schlemil	Bass
Dapertutto	Baritone
Pitichinaccio	Tenor
Antonia	Soprano
Crespel	Baritone
Franz	Tenor
Dr. Miracle	Baritone
Spirit voice	Soprano
Stella	Soprano
Muse	Soprano

SAMSON AND DELILAH

by Camille Saint-Saëns

Samson	Tenor
Delilah	Mezzo-soprano
Abimelech	Bass
High priest	Baritone
Old Hebrew	Bass

BORIS GODUNOFF

by Modest Moussorgsky

Boris Godunoff . . . . *Bass*
Prince Schouïsky . . . . *Tenor*
Tchelkaloff . . . . *Baritone*
Feodor . . . . *Mezzo-soprano*
Xenia . . . . *Soprano*
Pimenn . . . . *Bass*
Grigori . . . . *Tenor*
Hostess . . . . *Mezzo-soprano*
Varlaam . . . . *Bass*
Missaïl . . . . *Tenor*
Captain . . . . *Bass*
Nurse . . . . *Contralto*
Simpleton . . . . *Tenor*
Two Jesuit priests . . . . *Basses*
Marina . . . . *Soprano*
Rangoni . . . . *Bass*

HÄNSEL AND GRETEL

by Engelbert Humperdinck

Hänsel . . . . *Mezzo-soprano*
Gretel . . . . *Soprano*
Mother . . . . *Mezzo-soprano*
Father . . . . *Baritone*
Sandman . . . . *Soprano*
Dewman . . . . *Soprano*
Witch . . . . *Mezzo-soprano*

MANON LESCAUT

by Giacomo Puccini

Manon	Soprano
Des Grieux	Tenor
Edmondo	Tenor
Lescaut	Baritone
Geronte	Bass
Innkeeper	Bass
Dancing master	Tenor
Lamplighter	Tenor
Captain	Bass

ANDREA CHÉNIER

by Umberto Giordano

Andrea Chénier	Tenor
Gérard	Baritone
Madeleine	Soprano
Major-domo	Baritone
Countess de Coigny	Mezzo-soprano
Bersi	Mezzo-soprano
Abbé	Tenor
Fléville	Baritone
Mathieu	Baritone
Roucher	Baritone or bass
The spy	Tenor
Madelon	Mezzo-soprano
Fouquier-Tinville	Bass
The judge	Bass
Schmidt	Baritone or bass

LOUISE

by Gustave Charpentier

Louise . . . . *Soprano*
Mother . . . . *Contralto*
Father . . . . *Baritone or bass*
Julien . . . . *Tenor*
Milk woman, paper girl, coal-gatherer, scavenger, noctambulist, ragman, seamstresses, Father of Fools, and other people of Paris

PELLÉAS AND MÉLISANDE

by Claude Debussy

Golaud . . . . *Baritone*
Mélisande . . . . *Soprano*
Pelléas . . . . *Tenor*
Geneviève . . . . *Contralto*
Arkel . . . . *Bass*
Yniold . . . . *Soprano*
Physician . . . . *Bass*

BIOGRAPHICAL NOTES

WOLFGANG AMADEUS MOZART was born in Salzburg, Austria, on January 27, 1756. Even as a child he was a skilled performer on the harpsichord, as well as a distinguished composer in almost every musical form. In 1782 he went to live in Vienna, and that city was his home until his death on December 5, 1791.

LUDWIG VAN BEETHOVEN was born in Bonn, Germany, on December 16, 1770. When he was twenty-one he went to Vienna and was soon prominent in the musical life of the city as a composer, conductor, and performer. He died in Vienna on March 26, 1827.

CARL MARIA VON WEBER was born in Oldenburg, Germany, on November 18, 1786. After studying music in Salzburg, Munich, and Vienna, he devoted himself to conducting and composing operas. He died in London on June 5, 1826.

VINCENZO BELLINI was born in Catania, Sicily, on November 3, 1801. While studying at the Naples Conservatory he composed his first opera, and within a few years he was one of the most successful composers of his day. He died in Puteaux, France, on September, 23, 1835.

RICHARD WAGNER was born in Leipzig, Germany, on May 22, 1813. As a composer, he was largely self-taught. After conducting for several German opera companies, he went to Paris, where he completed two operas that were performed in Germany. They were *Rienzi* and *The Flying Dutchman*, and they led to his eventual success. Wagner died on February 13, 1883, while he and his wife were visiting Venice.

GIUSEPPE VERDI was born in La Roncole, Italy, on October 10, 1813. He was one of the most prolific of all opera composers. When his first opera was produced he was twenty-six, and he completed his last opera in his eightieth year. He died in Milan on January 27, 1901.

BEDRICH SMETANA was born in Litomischl, Bohemia, on March 2, 1824. When he was twenty he went to Prague to study music and within a few years he had become a successful pianist and comoposer. In 1856 he moved to Gothenburg, Sweden, and continued his musical career. Five years later he returned to Prague, where he was welcomed as a leader in the musical life of Prague. He was Bohemia's first important composer of national operas. He died in Prague on May 12, 1884.

AMILCARE PONCHIELLI was born in Paderno, Italy, on August 31, 1834. He studied music at the Milan Conservatory and afterward became an organist and the leader of a band. He composed several successful operas, then returned to the Milan Conservatory as a teacher. He died in Milan on January 16, 1886.

LÉO DELIBES was born in St. Germain du Val, France, on February 21, 1836. He attended the Paris Conservatory, then became a church organist and, later, direc-

tor of an opera chorus. He was widely known as a composer of ballets and operas. He died in Paris on January
16, 1891.

JACQUES OFFENBACH was born in Cologne, Germany, on June 20, 1819. He studied at the Paris Conservatory and afterward was a cellist in the orchestra of the
Paris Opéra-Comique. He became famous for his comic
operas. Late in his career he composed a serious opera,
The Tales of Hoffmann, but he did not live to see it produced. He died in Paris on October 4, 1880.

CAMILLE SAINT-SAËNS was born in Paris on October
9, 1835. He studied music privately and at the Paris Conservatory. He was an organist, concert pianist, and conductor, as well as a composer in almost every musical form.
On December 16, 1921, he died during a visit to Algiers.

MODEST MOUSSORGSKY was born in Karevo, Russia,
on March 21, 1839. He served in the army, then turned
seriously to composing. To earn a living, he worked as a
government clerk, and composed music in the time left
from his regular employment. He died in St. Petersburg
on March 28, 1881.

ENGELBERT HUMPERDINCK was born in Seigburg,
Germany, on September 1, 1854. He was in his middle
twenties before he decided to make music his profession.
He studied composition in Cologne and Munich. On a trip
to Italy he met Richard Wagner and later became his
assistant. Humperdinck died in Neusterlitz, Germany, on
September 27, 1921.

GIACOMO PUCCINI was born in Lucca, Italy, on December 22, 1858. He studied at the Milan Conservatory, where one of his teachers was the composer, Amilcare Ponchielli. Except for a few youthful compositions, all Puccini's works were for the operatic stage. He died in Brussels on November 29, 1924.

UMBERTO GIORDANO was born in Foggia, Italy, on August 27, 1867. While a student at Naples Conservatory, he composed his first opera, which showed so much promise that a music publisher commissioned him to compose a second. His fourth opera, *Andrea Chénier,* brought him success and world-wide recognition. He died in Milan on November 12, 1948.

GUSTAVE CHARPENTIER was born in Dieuze, France, on June 25, 1860. He studied music in France and Italy. Throughout his career he worked for social reform. He died in Paris on February 18, 1956.

CLAUDE DEBUSSY was born in Saint-Germain-en-Laye, France, on August 22, 1862. He was a student at the Paris Conservatory, and later he studied in Rome. He is well known for his orchestral and piano works and for his opera, *Pelléas and Mélisande.* He died in Paris on March 25, 1918.

INDEX

ABOUT THE AUTHOR

Clyde Robert Bulla was born near King City, Missouri. His formal education began in a one-room schoolhouse, where he wrote his first stories and composed his first songs.

Music, and opera in particular, has always been an important part of Mr. Bulla's life. He has previously written two books which tell the stories of well-known operas in a simple and direct manner:

Stories of Favorite Operas and *The Ring and the Fire:* Stories from Wagner's Nibelung Operas.

Mr. Bulla lives in Los Angeles, California.

ABOUT THE ILLUSTRATOR

Joseph Low was born in Coraopolis, Pennsylvania; attended schools in Oak Park, Illinois; and studied at the University of Illinois. Finding that he could learn more of what he wanted by studying on his own in museums and libraries, he pursued his interest in the graphic arts, teaching himself the skills that he needed and acquiring the necessary tools, type, and a press.

After spending some time at the Art Students League in New York City, Mr. Low taught graphic arts at Indiana University for three years. He is a printer and publisher, with his own Eden Hill Press, as well as an artist.

His work has been exhibited in museums across the United States, in England, in South America, the Orient, and in Europe. He lives in Connecticut with his wife and two daughters.